SEAT
Food Crawls

Grubbin' Seattle

TOURING the NEIGHBORHOODS
ONE BITE & LIBATION at a TIME

Globe
Pequot

GUILFORD, CONNECTICUT

D0546732

Globe
Pequot

An imprint of The Rowman & Littlefield Publishing Group, Inc.
4501 Forbes Blvd., Ste. 200
Lanham, MD 20706
www.rowman.com

Distributed by NATIONAL BOOK NETWORK

British Library Cataloguing in Publication Information available

Library of Congress Cataloging-in-Publication Data available

ISBN 978-1-4930-3884-8 (paperback)
ISBN 978-1-4930-3885-5 (e-book)

∞™ The paper used in this publication meets the minimum require-
ments of American National Standard for Information Sciences—Perma-
nence of Paper for Printed Library Materials, ANSI/NISO Z39.48-1992

Printed in the United States of America

Contents

Introduction

THE 206 IS KNOWN FOR ITS CHRONIC RAIN, coffee drinking, and Nirvana head-banging, but the food scene here is a little slice of heaven. What was once a slower-paced grungy city is now a fast-moving, tech-booming metropolis. Home to powerhouses like Amazon, Microsoft, Starbucks, and Nordstrom, there's now a huge hipster/techie population that commands a city with top-tier dining options, from dive bars to elegant multicourse dinner spots. The bountiful Pacific Northwest is made up of water, mountains, and lush green lands, which are ideal for farming, meaning we've been about that farm-to-table life long before it became an overused buzzword. Seattle's found its niche in highlighting the special ingredients that are produced in our unique climate, from (literally) boatloads of fresh seafood to the juiciest Washington apples to locally foraged mushrooms and our famous Rainier cherries. The list of foods we do best goes on and on.

A longtime thriving port city (dating back to 1851), Seattle has welcomed people from all around the world who bring with them their unique food traditions, which have shaped Seattle into one of the most diverse and dynamic food cultures in the United States. While always on the forefront of trends, there's plenty of exciting places for you to hit, but don't miss out on classics like Pike Place Chowder and our favorite burgers from Dick's Drive-In. Each neighborhood has something different to offer, and these little pieces make up the puzzle that is the beautiful (and delicious) city of Seattle. I'm stoked to be your guide as we eat our way through these neighborhoods and their killer restaurants. We'll slurp oysters by the dozen at Westward, tackle a tableful of tapas at Pintxo, and indulge in enormous slices of cake at Deep Sea Sugar & Salt in Georgetown. To show you exactly what your experience would look like, I've shot this book entirely on my iPhone. Now it's your turn to explore Seattle, one shameless food photo at a time!

Follow the Icons

 If you eat something outrageous and don't take a photo for Instagram, did you really eat it? These restaurants feature dishes that are Instagram famous. The foods must be seen (and snapped) to be believed, and luckily they taste as good as they look!

 Cheers to a fabulous night out in Seattle! These spots add a little glam to your grub and are perfect for marking a special occasion.

 Follow this icon when you're crawling for cocktails. This symbol points out the establishments that are best known for their great drinks. The food never fails here, but be sure to come thirsty, too!

 This icon means that sweet treats are ahead. Bring your sweet tooth to these spots for dessert first (or second or third).

 Seattle is for brunch. Look for this icon when crawling with a crew that needs sweet and savory (or an excuse to drink before noon).

Capitol Hill

What The Hipsters Eat

FOREVER HOME OF THE GORGEOUS GAYS, CAPITOL HILL is the queen of Seattle. This energetic neighborhood is stacked with super-hip bars, eateries, java houses, and gay clubs, with no shortage of tech nerds or moody hipsters. During the day, people bop around the endless blocks of Capitol Hill (always with coffee in hand) checking out its boutiques, salons, parks, bookstores, and, on Sunday, the Broadway Farmers' Market. But truth be told, this neighborhood really comes alive at night. Known for being the epicenter of the city's music (the birthplace of the grunge movement), entertainment, and art scene, this is the place for living out loud. I mean, this neighborhood is so cool it even has its own music festival. Every July, locals and visitors flock to these rainbow-painted streets for the Capitol Hill Block Party studded with big names and artists native to Seattle. Capitol Hill on the weekend defines "lit" —and at times, it's too lit. But if you're looking for a good time, this neighborhood really is your spot. Just beware of blacked-out college kids and armies of chicks who can't handle their booze.

THE CAPITOL HILL CRAWL

1. **THE WANDERING GOOSE,** 403 15TH AVE. E, SEATTLE, THEWANDERINGGOOSE.COM, (206) 323-9938

2. **STATESIDE,** 300 E. PIKE ST., SEATTLE, STATESIDESEATTLE.COM, (206) 557-7273

3. **TACOS CHUKIS,** 219 BROADWAY E, SEATTLE, FACEBOOK.COM/ TACOSCHUKIS, NO PHONE

4. **NUE,** 1519 14TH AVE., SEATTLE, NUESEATTLE.COM, (206) 257-0312

5. **HELLO ROBIN,** 522 19TH AVE. E, SEATTLE, HELLOROBINCOOKIES.COM, (206) 735-7970

6. **DICK'S DRIVE-IN,** 115 BROADWAY E, SEATTLE, DDIR.COM, (206) 323-1300

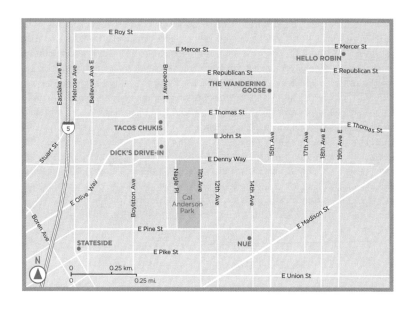

1

BISCUITS FOR BREAKFAST
AT THE WANDERING GOOSE

Biscuit lovers use caution—this Southern-influenced cafe nestled in the heart of North Capitol Hill will ruin all other biscuits forever. Chef and owner Heather Earnhardt is warming our hearts and our bellies with this soft and flaky perfection, adorned with infinite house-made fixins like butter, jam, mustard, fried chicken, pickles and honey. And the goodness only just starts at biscuits. The menu is studded with Southern classics like hush puppies, a mean fried oyster hash, grits, and pimento mac and cheese—all of which you can feast on during their popular Fried Chicken Dinners on Fridays. You'll feel like a kid in candy store when you lock eyes with the pastry case chockfull of cookies, layer cakes, and biscuit cinnamon rolls. There truly is no sight more beautiful. If you're counting carbs, then you're in "Big Trouble." This biscuit sandwich is piled high with peanut butter, bacon, bananas, and Heather's very own honey, which she sources from her rooftop beehives and is nice enough to sell by the jar. If you're feeling savory, the Sawmill is a gravy junkie's dream come true—the fluffiest biscuit stuffed with properly spiced

The birthday cake is to die for. Grab a slice to go!

fried chicken and cheese, drenched in a rich sausage gravy. There's a 100 percent chance you'll lick the plate clean. Sure to please carnivores and veg-heads alike is the veggie hash, with seasonal veggies and potatoes. Ask what the "squeeze of the day" is, as you'll appreciate some fresh juice while scarfing down these biscuits. Since this space is pretty tiny, weekend crowds can be a bit unbearable, so if you don't want go get stuck in a line out the door, I suggest you hit it on a weekday morning. Arguably Seattle's best spot for early morning grub, this sweet cafe should be at the top of your list!

2 BRUNCHIN' WORLDWIDE AT STATESIDE

Seattle knows a good thing when it's got one; that's why every weekend there's a mob of hangry brunchers waiting to snag a table at Eric Johnson's Vietnamese fusion, tropical-themed flavor house. This is not your typical brunch stop, and thank god for that. He's putting a Vietnamese spin on classic brunch dishes that are listed alongside traditional fare like fresh rolls, soups, and noodles. These are #eeeeats you most likely haven't had before, but that's because this is next-level brunching. To start, Crispy Duck Fresh Rolls and a colorful Coconut Yogurt Parfait, best eaten with a mug full of coffee and a Lychee Boba Mimosa. Next, order the Eggs Bao'nedict, a golden, steamed bun filled with Canadian bacon and topped with poached eggs, hollandaise, and pork floss—because hot and steamy buns are life. The famed Hong Kong Style Charcoal Waffle is crucial if you're into "doing it for the gram," or if you simply love waffles. A jet-black waffle served with coconut-pandan syrup, mango jam, shaved almonds, and the optional scoop of coconut-pandan ice cream (a total no-brainer). And wait, the sweet brunch items don't stop there: The Cassia Brioche French Toast with vanilla-bean whipped cream and caramelized bananas is too sexy to be ignored . . . she definitely deserves a spot on the table. Stateside for brunch

TIP

Their equally popular sister bar, Foreign National, is attached at the hip right next door. They serve excellent cocktails and bomb Asian fusion bar snacks like Cheeseburger Bao Buns.

is kind of like the perfect tropical getaway from Seattle's gross and chronic rain. Get here right at opening—the food at this hot spot tastes so much better when you don't have to wait.

3

TONS OF TACOS FOR LUNCH AT TACOS CHUKIS

Come one taco lover, come all taco lovers! We Seattleites hold this tiny taqueria near and dear to our hearts. Somewhat hidden on the second story of an indoor mall on East Broadway, you'll find Seattle's favorite tacos. Which means this joint is popular, but don't be shook when you see the mosh pit of people—they clear out fast. At the stupidly low price of $1.90, these fantastically simple tacos come with your choice of grilled protein, cilantro, onion, salsa, and guacamole served over fresh corn tortillas. The menu lists other items like tortas and quesadillas—these cost a bit more than the tacos but will also leave you smiling ear to ear. The bread used for the tortas is crunchy yet soft, and the house taco will blow your mind: an adobada pork taco with melted cheese, guacamole, and grilled pineapple. Who would've thought pineapple on a taco could be so life changing? Sweet, spicy, meaty—it works. Another one of my go-to bites is the mulita—the taco's hotter and cheesier older sister. It's basically a mini quesadilla made with corn tortillas instead of flour (I can't resist the crispy cheesy edges). Throw one of those on the order and charge it to the game. This spot makes for a cheap and promising lunch date—twenty bucks will fill two people up easily. The prices are low, but the flavors are on point. Chances are you'll hop back in line once you finish what's on your plate, and there's definitely zero shame in that. If you're smart, you'll order a baby burrito to go and wash it all down with some horchata or agua fresca.

4 EATING NEW THINGS FOR DINNER AT NUE

Nue is hands down the most unique restaurant in Seattle. Owner Chris Cvetkovich and his team travel the world, hunting down the greatest eats the streets have to offer. Each of their globally inspired dishes is sure to take you out of your comfort zone in the most insanely delicious way possible—like Thai Water Beetles that taste freakishly similar to Jolly Ranchers (this was a brave, brave moment for me).

But slow your roll; this worldwide culinary adventure has only just begun. Straight off the street grills of Barbados comes the oh-so-tender pork tails with jerk glaze, cilantro, and lime. Basically genius is the South African Bunny Chow (no, we're not eating Thumper), which is essentially Indian chicken masala in a box of bread. The soft insides soak up the flavor of the masala while the outside stays crunchy. Our next attraction is the epic leaning tower of Chengdu Spicy Jumbo Chicken Wings with tongue-numbing

green Szechuan peppercorns, fish sauce, lime, Thai chile, and a refreshing mint finish. Just one hit of the Pineapple Cornbread with toasted coconut and you'll be hooked. Throughout this exciting feast you'll find yourself distracted by the rad, mishmash decor including Chinese lanterns along the bar and walls lined with shelves holding random trinkets they've accumulated abroad. It's like a real-life game of I spy. The cocktail menu offers a spin on classics, like the Nue Fashioned with rye, ginger molasses, and orange bitters, and unique sips like the Beetle Juice, which is a vodka cocktail infused with our fruity beetle friend mentioned above. They also have a killer brunch menu, served every single day from 10 a.m. to 3 p.m. Nue is not for picky eaters, so call your down-ass homie and get weird.

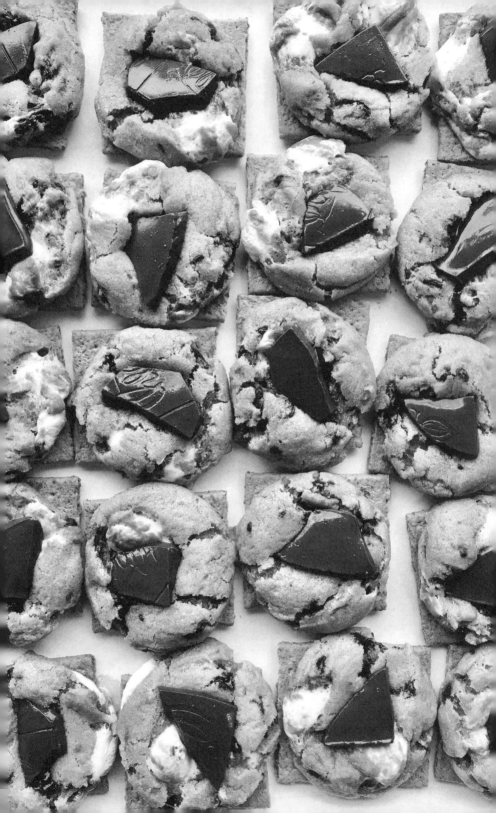

BIRTHDAY CAKE

5 HELLO ROBIN FOR DESSERT IS MANDATORY

Cookies and ice cream—a match made in sugar heaven. But this seriously cute treat shop isn't selling just any cookies and ice cream. The cookie queen herself, Robin Wehl, pairs her fresh-baked cookies with the ice-cream voodoo of Molly Moon. These besties decided to team up, and the rest is history. We're talking crazy delicious combos like a scoop of salted caramel ice cream sandwiched between two Birthday Cake cookies. Do we have any Macklemore fans out there? Even if you're not a fan of Seattle's hip-hop king, you'll be a fan of his cookie counterpart, the Mackels'more, a s'more cookie sitting atop a graham cracker and finished with giant chunks of Theo's Chocolate (Theo's is another local sweet gem, but we'll get to that later). I'm a Hello Robin veteran, so my order never changes: a scoop of strawberry ice cream hugged by two Flourless Mexican Chocolate cookies. That's how it's done. So many bomb af cookie options your head might start to spin: Orange Habanero Chocolate Chip, Salted Butterscotch, Milk Chocolate Lavender, and Lemon Glazed Poppy Seed just to name a few. Stop by Friday for some fresh challah bread or during the weekend for an obligatory cinnamon roll. This cookie kingdom is open till 10 p.m. on weekdays and 11 p.m. on weekends, so you really have no excuse not to check it out.

> **TIP**
>
> If you're not feeling an entire ice-cream sandwich, you can order an open-faced sammy (one cookie plus a scoop).

6 LATE NIGHT MUNCHIES AT DICK'S DRIVE-IN

Dick's Drive-In is a religion to Seattleites—it's like our very own In-N-Out Burger or Shake Shack. This legendary fast-food staple is open till 2 a.m. and has been satisfying drunchies since 1954. A Seattle visit is not complete without a Dick's run. Always fresh burgers, fries, and shakes are ordered and inhaled in your car or among the masses of hungry, drunk, and/or stoned customers. The small menu lists five different burgers, and no substitutions are

allowed. They've been serving up these locally sourced meaty morsels for decades, so there's no need to mess with perfection. Whether you order a Dick's Deluxe (two ⅛-pound grilled patties with melted cheese, lettuce, mayonnaise, and pickle relish) or a cheeseburger (a single ⅛-pound grilled patty and melted cheese with ketchup and mustard), you'll be a happy camper. Pro tip: If you absolutely must have ketchup on your Deluxe, order a side and top that baby off. There's no better nightcap than a Deluxe, extra cheeseburger, fries (hand-cut and hot) with a side of tartar, and a strawberry shake. If you're feeling frisky, upgrade that shake to a vanilla sundae with hot fudge and blackberry compote. The best and most satisfying part of the Dick's experience is being handed your bag of burgs only seconds after ordering. This old-school establishment is a well-oiled machine. All other burger shops are incomparable; not sure if it's the nostalgia speaking, but for years, Dick's Drive-In has kept the prices low and the burgers ridiculously tasty. When it comes to late-night eats, nothing screams Seattle more than this OG establishment.

There was only one other fast-food restaurant in Seattle when they opened up shop in 1954.

Fremont

Gettin' Funky in Fremont: Fried Pickles at 1 a.m.

IT DOESN'T GET MUCH FUNKIER THAN FREMONT. Since 1970 locals have called this peculiar neighborhood "the center of the universe." With a ton of personality (probably the most of any Seattle neighborhood), Fremont sure feels like the center point of Seattle—there's no place quite like it. Where else can you find a troll under a bridge, naked bike riders, a chocolate factory, and a giant Lenin statue? There's a lot to do and see here. Unique, independently owned boutiques, cute coffee shops, a groovy vintage mall, and an awesome flea market inside a parking garage during the Sunday Farmer's Market ($15 Levis are a major score). You don't want to miss the Solstice Parade in June; it's the best people-watching opportunity, like ever. Hundreds of cyclists covered in nothing but paint, tons of hippies, puppets, and drunks flock to the streets to celebrate the start of summer. Sunny Fremont days are best spent throwing back copious amounts of oysters and rosé on the shores of Lake Union at Westward or brunching on Pablo y Pablo's perfect patio. The food scene holds its own and only continues to grow with something for everyone, even your vegan cousin who thinks she's saving the world one leaf of kale at a time. The bars are fun, and the night crowd can get real weird. The Ballroom is where you'll find the entire University of Washington Greek system, and The Backdoor is where you go to hide from those people. The many craft breweries and cideries also offer a chiller vibe. There's live music almost every night to dance yourself clean to and tons of outdoor drinking spaces for those beloved warm summer nights.

THE FREMONT CRAWL

1. **ROXY'S DINER**, 462 N. 36TH ST., SEATTLE, PASTRAMISANDWICH.COM, (206) 632-3963

2. **PABLO Y PABLO**, 1605 N. 34TH ST., SEATTLE, PABLOYPABLO.COM, (206) 973-3505

3. **FREMONT BOWL**, 4258 FREMONT AVE N, STE. #4262, FREMONTBOWL.COM, (206) 504-3095

4. **WESTWARD**, 2501 N. NORTHLAKE WAY, SEATTLE, WESTWARDSEATTLE .COM, (206) 552-8215

5. **THEO'S CHOCOLATE FACTORY & RETAIL**, 3400 PHINNEY AVE. N, SEATTLE, THEOSCHOCOLATE.COM, (206) 632-5100

6. **THE BACKDOOR**, 462 N. 36TH ST., SEATTLE, BACKDOORATROXYS.COM, (206) 632-7322

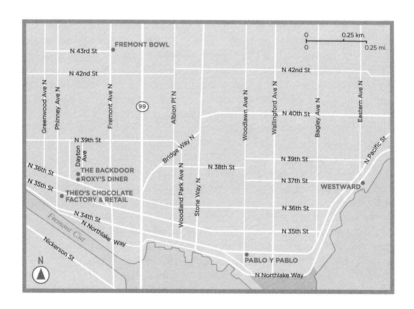

1 ENDLESS BAGELS AND MIMOSAS FOR BREAKFAST AT ROXY'S DINER

When you're still riding that wave from last night, Roxy's Diner doesn't judge, and neither do I. This East Coast–inspired diner serves all-day breakfast and Jewish deli fare that's sure to nurse your hangover. The place is unpretentious and casual, so if you roll in wearing sweatpants and a crop top, no one will care. A fun atmosphere, waiters who can crack a joke, bottomless coffee and surprisingly cheap booze. If $3 mimosas won't get the squad out of bed, then $3.95 bagel sandwiches might do the trick. These bagels are made in-house daily and can

be dressed up or down to your liking. Taking home a dozen wouldn't be a bad idea, and ordering the lox would be an even better one. They make a solid pastrami Reuben, and said pastrami tastes even better in a scramble. A challah french toast to soak up last night's regret (add bananas and chocolate) and matzoh ball soup for additional emotional support. I'm not sure how grandma would feel about Roxy's Latke Sandwich, but it's something that anybody who cares about latkes should take seriously. The menu is freakishly long, and everything is

TIP

Ask the server about their famous "Restraining Order" and follow through. It's a shot of whiskey followed by a slap to the face. Yes, you pay to be slapped.

served with a side of sass (which I love). From the staff to the colorful decor, Roxy's Diner is totally quirky. Unless you're a fun hater, you'll always leave satisfied and with a big ol' smile on your face. For those going full Sunday-Funday mode, this is the ultimate precursor to treasure hunting at the Fremont farmers' market.

2 BURRITO BRUNCH DATES AT PABLO Y PABLO

Pablo y Pablo is showing Seattle how to do not only brunch but Mexican food in general. Plus, I can't think of a more vibes place to brunch on a sunny Saturday morning—all of the feels and all of the churros. The outdoor patio will seat everyone, no problem. Drinks are on point, food is crave-worthy, and parking (free, might I add) isn't a struggle. The chilaquiles are described as "the. best. damn. hang. over. cure. ever," and they ain't lying.

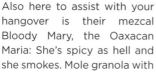

Also here to assist with your hangover is their mezcal Bloody Mary, the Oaxacan Maria: She's spicy as hell and she smokes. Mole granola with almond milk—is it savory, is it sweet? It's both and I demand a bag to go. Breakfast tacos that you won't find at your local taco truck; bacon with cheesy eggs and jalapeño salsa, fried chicken atop a mini jalapeño pancake taco (favorite) and one drenched in habanero hollandaise. The hot sauce is served in a little dropper bottle that is freakin' adorable and fun to use. Breakfast burrito connoisseurs, this one's for you: cheesy eggs, potatoes, guac, salsa, roasted onion, peppers, and crema lovingly wrapped up like your mom's first child. The challah french toast with horchata whipped cream, fresh berries, and vanilla maple syrup is everything you've ever wanted french toast to be. Go the extra carb mile and order the churros with rich, velvety xocalatl chocolate sauce. Sexy like the churros is the interior, light and bright thanks to the many windows and the "cantina meets Anthropologie Spring/Summer 2019" decor, you'll feel chic af just being here.

3

KEEPING LUNCH FRESH AT FREMONT BOWL

It's no secret that Seattle has an excess of poke options. In 2017, Fremont Bowl popped up out of nowhere and since then we haven't thought twice about the newest poke place. The word spread fast about these uber fresh, monstrous bowls of raw fish, katsu, and teriyaki, and it seriously seems like it was overnight fame for this Japanese comfort-food joint. Travel a half mile up Fremont Avenue and you'll find bowls on bowls. About 13 of them to be exact, the most popular being the chirashi bowl. Closely comparable to poke, but clearly a standout. A traditional dish of raw fatty tuna, salmon, yellowtail, albacore, shrimp, fresh-water eel, masago with wasabi, and yuzu kosho on top of rice flavored with rice vinegar. Chirashi means "scattered," but each piece of colorful sushi-grade sashimi is put perfectly in its place.

They do not skimp on the fish, and for only $15 you have to wonder if these crazy people are even turning a profit. Their house-made soy sauce is quite the treat. If you're feeling good ol' poke, they have that, too. If katsu is your jam, there's both pork and chicken (with the option to mix the two). Chicken teriyaki is on the menu, and it's up to Seattle standards. The small space features a counter with Japanese snacks and canned beverages, a line of close-set tables, and an open kitchen. Dine in or out, your choice. But I advise all first-timers to wait for a seat and try their dine-in-only dish, Aburi Sake Don. Melt-in-your-mouth seared salmon with fresh wasabi and yuzu kosho. The smoke from the seared salmon seeps into the bowl, and drool will be coming out of both sides of your mouth. Don't bother trying another poke place; Fremont Bowl is right here and slaying more than just poke.

4 WALKING IN A DINNER WONDERLAND AT WESTWARD

Westward is Seattle's summer anthem. A beachfront restaurant on the north shores of Lake Union with a firepit, rows of Adirondack chairs, and striped umbrellas overlooking the lake and city skyline. This slice of paradise is where we congregate when the sun makes an appearance. It feels like a true escape from the tech-bubble madness and traffic jams. The menu features fairy tale–like Mediterranean-inspired dishes, a full-service oyster bar, and rosé that flows like water. The nautically themed interior is straight out of a Wes Anderson film, super whimsical and well thought out. It's safe to say Westward could be Seattle's most Instagrammed restaurant, and nobody's getting sick of seeing this content. If you aren't lucky enough to score a beach chair, a seat at the oyster bar is the next best thing. Watch the mother shuckers get to work plating up the unique varieties of fresh local oysters.

TIP

Oysters are $2 during happy hour—let's get shucked up!

The hearth fire is the center of attention and where the magic happens. Just thinking about the braised lamb has me tearing up. It's served with house-made roti, tzatziki, and pure joy—you break it all apart to assemble your own gyro. The Wood-Fired Gigante Beans are also a real crowd-pleaser—literal gigantic beans in a skillet of thick tomato sauce and feta. If they didn't cost as much as a movie ticket, I'd order about 10 more. Octopus served atop a hot pink sauce of some sort—whoa. A scallop crudo so pretty you'll start to feel insecure. A whole rainbow trout that's deboned tableside, most likely by your attractive server (shallow? maybe). One butterscotch pot de crème and another glass of rosé, please and thank you!

5 BINGE ON CHOCOLATE SAMPLES AT THEO'S CHOCOLATE FACTORY & RETAIL

When strolling through Fremont you'll often catch a whiff of chocolaty goodness followed by the usual "omg, do you smell that?" What you're smelling is our very own chocolate factory, similar to Wonka's, minus the Oompa Loompas, candy trees and chocolate river. Upon entering the retail store, you'll fall into a chocolate-tasting daze. Theo's was the first organic and fair trade–certified chocolate factory to hit North America, and they're damn proud of that. They want you to taste every single one of their ethically sourced chocolates and learn all there is to know about their bean-to-bar process. This is why they offer factory tours, where you'll eat a ton of chocolate and get a close look at how it's made. Tours are $10 and last about an hour—definitely a must-do Fremont activity. Besides, it's almost impossible and plain stupid to walk by Theo's without stopping in for some free chocolate. They have their classic bars: salted almond, chili, turmeric spice, black rice quinoa crunch, and a handful of creative seasonals. The dark-chocolate peanut-butter cups are a weakness. But my absolute favorite confection of theirs is the Big Daddy, a dilf you need to meet. Layers of graham cracker, vanilla-infused caramel, and fluffy marshmallow all enrobed in dark chocolate. You can purchase these individually or by the three-pack at their truffle counter. Let the chocolate binge commence!

> **TIP**
>
> Every third Thursday of the month they offer a free tour to the public at 4:30 p.m. Seats for the tour are released two months in advance!

THE BACK THE DOOR

Craft Cocktails
Fine Food

BAR TO 2AM
KITCHEN TO 11PM

Happy Hour 5-7 DAILY

6

THE COOL CROWD HANGS OUT LATE AT THE BACKDOOR

Everyone loves to be in on a secret—that's why taking your friends to a bar through an unmarked door is a "speakeasy" way to impress them. In the parking lot next to Roxy's Diner you'll find The Backdoor, opening up to a colorful and eclectic Prohibition-themed bar. No password needed, but this lively place fills up. A jazz-age vibe with high ceilings and flapper/musician mural–covered walls. The open room has plenty of tables scattered throughout and a majestic bar in the middle of it all. The small nook by the entrance will catch your eye—a pink open-faced booth beneath Victorian crystal chandeliers and surrounded by mirror-lined walls . . . this is prime real estate for a girls' night out. The bartenders are just as lovable—whipping up craft cocktails with house-infused booze and shrubs. They have a shit ton of cocktails to choose from, and if you cannot choose, ask your bartender to surprise you at three different price points. Once you decide on a nightcap beverage (or two), the late-night bites decision making will be a bit more of a no-brainer. A juicy Animal Style burger that will crush any In-N-Out craving you may have. I honestly can't get enough of their fried pickles—these crunchy delights are served in a mug with a side of house-made ranch and will be gone in an instant. Other irresistible snacks are the fried oysters, curried cauliflower, and churro bites with fudge. This hidden gem in the heart of Fremont is the coolest spot for late-night drinks and snacks, or a great place to start out the night.

Pioneer Square

Underground Tours & Schnitzel

AS THE OLDEST NEIGHBORHOOD IN SEATTLE, HISTORIC PIONEER Square goes way, way back to 1852. The buildings have been somewhat restored, keeping their exposed brick, and this is exactly what makes Pioneer Square so charming. It's just a stone's throw away from Downtown and the home of the Seattle Mariners and the Seahawks. 'Hawks fans are pretty passionate, so things can get really rambunctious around here during football season. The aesthetically pleasing Occidental Square is the heart of it all; trees provide shade for the outdoor tables and seats, ping-pong tables, food trucks, and art installations. A sweet place to sip on coffee from The London Plane and people watch. And at night, the hanging lights make for a dreamy setting. A handful of cute restaurants, cafes, and shops sit on these cobblestone streets. On Washington Street, right next door to Lady Yum Macarons is a rad vintage store called Bon Voyage. Grab a macaron and then get your shop on. Pioneer Square is totally artsy-fartsy and hosts an art walk, which includes free wine, every first Thursday of the month. Speaking of alcohol, the nightlife here can be either rowdy or romantic. Countless taverns, clubs, and sports bars to keep you from your regularly scheduled programming (Netflix in bed). Wildy enough, the original Seattle is underground, thanks to the gold rush and the great fire of 1889. It's as crazy as it sounds, and there's a lot more to it, so I recommend you take the famous Underground Tour. And yes, a fair amount of homeless reside in this neighborhood, but they're friendly, and this is their home, too. Don't let that be a reason not to check out this special part of Seattle.

THE PIONEER SQUARE CRAWL

1. **THE LONDON PLANE,** 300 OCCIDENTAL AVE. S, SEATTLE, THELONDONPLANESEATTLE.COM, (206) 624-1374

2. **ALTSTADT,** 209 1ST AVE. S, SEATTLE, ALTSTADTSEATTLE.COM, (206) 602-6442

3. **QUALITY ATHLETICS,** 121 S. KING ST., SEATTLE, QUALITYATHLETICS.COM, (206) 420-3015

4. **GIRIN,** 501 STADIUM PLACE S, SEATTLE, GIRINSEATTLE.COM, (206) 257-4259

5. **GOOD BAR,** 240 2ND AVE. S, SEATTLE, GOODBARSEATTLE.COM, (206) 624-2337

1

PINTEREST PERFECT BREAKFAST AT THE LONDON PLANE

Located in the oh-so-photogenic Occidental Square is Seattle's hipster oasis The London Plane. A beyond gorgeous space, elegant and airy with high ceilings and tall windows that let the very rare Seattle sun in. Part local goods grocer, flower workshop, bakery, and cafe, opening at 8 a.m. for weekday breakfast — an ideal opportunity to drop in and skip the weekend brunch crowd. A lovely place to zone out with coffee and pastry in hand. Treat your inner Alice in Wonderland to a slice of the pistachio cardamom cake. It's sprinkled with what looks to be tiny magical rose petals. You'll be satisfied with a handmade croissant or biscuit with cultured butter and preserves that change seasonally. If you're a three-meals-a-day type of girl, like me, there are some killer options that will fill you up. The menu lists an array of soups, salads and daily plates made of ingredients you've probably never heard of, but whatever you order is bound to be stunning. Prepare for an instant love connection with the Muhammara Toast, a sweet and smoky Middle Eastern spread made of red peppers, walnuts, and spices, topped with brussels sprouts, Gouda, and pomegranate. Avocado toast, who? One bite, two bite, six bites, gone. Another Middle Eastern–inspired dish hit out of the park—their baked eggs with spicy harissa and Urfa yogurt, served with thick slices of house-baked bread to mop up the marvelous tomato sauce and dunk into the soft yolks. You should strongly consider the merguez (lamb sausage) sandwich with harissa, gruyère, mint, and pickles.

Not in the mood for breakfast? Easy on the eyes and full of flavor are the rotating salad and roasted vegetable options. The restaurant also ferments its own kombucha in-house, because your gut deserves a little somethin' somethin'.

TIP

Their craveable sourdough is baked in-house and available by the loaf, so you should probably grab one to go.

2 DAS BOOTS FOR BRUNCH AT ALTSTADT

Bet you haven't brunched in a German beer hall before, and it's about time we change that. Having lived in Germany and cooked at one of its Michelin-starred restaurants, chef and owner Megan Coombes is introducing us Seattleites to traditional German fare. Pio Sq's Altstadt will win you over with their selection of reasonably priced German beers and reinvented classics from bratwurst and beyond. Beer for brunch, because when in Rome, right? Correction, when in Germany, right? The communal table seating makes this spot a choice option for pre-Hawks game brunch or when the whole squad annoyingly wants to brunch together. You're likely to be greeted by the sweet aroma of crepes and a dude aggressively kneading pretzel dough. The soft pretzels are heavenly: chewy with just the right amount of salt. They're served with spicy mustard and the optional addition of beer cheese (you need the beer cheese) and best enjoyed with a brew and or kraut Bloody Mary #turnuptheyeast. This just in: Schnitzel is the shit and makes a great foundation for day drinking. As do crepes, especially those filled with berry compote or cured salmon. And to wash that all down, you and your crew order Das Boot, a 4-liter boot filled with beer of your choice. Don't you dare let this bad boy hit the table; pass it around till not a drop is left. This is sure to make the Underground Tour—or whatever you have planned for that matter—more entertaining.

3 HOME-RUN LUNCHES AT QUALITY ATHLETICS

Don't let the name throw you—you won't find jockstraps for sale here, and it's certainly not your shitty neighborhood sports pub. Quality Athletics is upping not only the sports bar game but Seattle eats in general. They're performing culinary sorcery on your standard bar fare with international flavors and locally sourced ingredients (some from their own rooftop garden). Neighboring both CenturyLink and Safeco Field, it's easily one of the most crowded places during a Seattle sports game. The firepits on both sides of the patio are where you'll want to be. The interior tastefully follows a sports theme, with locker-lined walls, framed photos of sports legends, and trophies. And with a ton of screens for watching, this is a dope spot to catch a game—but let's be real, I come here for the food. This being my most-frequented grubbing hole, I have a long list of favorites. We'll start at the Loaded Al Pastor Fries, a mountain of fries topped with marinated pork shoulder, grilled pineapple slaw, cheese, cilantro, onion, jalapeño, and sour cream. And to really heat things up, we have the cheddar habanero waffle topped with a fried egg, fried chicken, and smoked maple syrup. You don't need to google "French food Seattle" to discover the city's best steak frites; you can find mouthwatering beefy goodness right here: a 10-ounce grass-fed New York strip steak dripping with lemon herb butter and hand-cut fries. Let me save you even more time and key you in on something else they're absolutely slaying—ramen. Ideally eaten on one

of our many gloomy days, their pork belly ramen is styled up with a sous vide egg, green onions, and house chile oil. Last but definitely not least is the Pizza Mac, cheesy shells of fresh pasta topped with pepperoni and green onions. Everything you love about pizza, eaten with a fork. Sports fan or not, Quality Athletics is the spot.

TIP

They brew their own lavender ginger beer, which is obviously ideal for their Build Your Own Mule.

4

KOREAN DELIGHTS FOR DINNER AT GIRIN

To find promising Korean food—like the really good stuff—one usually has to drive super north or south. Luckily, Girin is promising, really good, and not deep as hell. It's definitely fancier than anything you'd find in Lynnwood, but their innovative take on classic Korean dishes helps justify spending the few extra dollars. The restaurant itself is gorgeous and definitely nice enough for a night out with the future in-laws. Most of the menu is served ssam-style with bowls of leafy greens, garlic, and chiles for wrapping delicious meats. Selecting those meats is the hard part: wagyu gold-grade New York strip, grilled pork belly, kalbi (marinated and grilled short ribs), and the list continues. Flavorful small plates make up the other half of the menu. Probably the prettiest dish on the menu is Yukhwe: prosciutto-thin slices of raw beef with egg yolk, Asian pear, and pine nuts. Get that and a few others to start, because this is a family-style situation. The sweet and spicy gochujang wings, baby back ribs, and fried oysters are all very worthy of consumption. The kimchi jjigae soup is my absolute mood on just about any

fall or winter day. It's like medicine for my weather-depressed soul. Full send ahead because the dumplings are house made and worth the extra order. Pork, beef, or veggie, steamed or fried. You can get whatever you like *T.I. voice.* According to the owner, Steven Han, this is "drinking food," so you'd be doing it all wrong if you didn't order a kettle of makgeolli. This traditional Korean fermented rice beverage will sneak up on ya, and Girin is the only place in America licensed to brew it. For those on the hunt for a quick bite before the game, most of the small plates and oysters can be found for cheap on their happy hour menu.

5

GREATEST LATE NIGHT AT GOOD BAR

Good Bar is just that—a really good bar. This quintessential Seattle tavern specializes in awesome service, high-end bar bites and artisinal sips. It's inside an old bank originally built in 1900, showing off Pioneer Square's historic charm. It feels swanky, but your Seahawks attire is encouraged, and it's somewhat under the radar so your Tinder date will think you're cooler than you actually are. The bar is centered around an extensive beer list, short but sweet wine program and a well-executed cocktail menu. The bartenders really give a shit and will impress the hell out of you with their creative potions. The Milk Money is creamy and vibrant in both color and taste: Irish cream, matcha, absinthe, anisette, and fresh mint. The "Not Into Yoga" is far more rewarding (and cheaper) than an hour-long stretch session in a sweat chamber—you'll absolutely die for this tropical bevvy made of Puerto Rican rum, cashew feni (an Indian liquor), cream of coconut, and fresh pineapple. The late-night menu of your dreams is served till 2 a.m. on weekends. If your table doesn't have food on it you're making a big mistake—build your own charcuterie board and share a few plates. They've hit it out of the park with their signature sloppy joe—it's one of the messiest crave-worthy bites you'll find in the city: stout beer–reduced Painted Hills beef sweetened with tomato and warmed up with cinnamon, drizzled with a roasted onion aioli and spilling out of a toasted Macrina ciabatta

bun. This masterpiece must be ordered alongside the fingerling potatoes—they're meant for each other. Sliced fingerlings roasted to a T, sprinkled with Maldon salt, and served with a smoked paprika potato-salad aioli for dipping. The roasted mussels don't suck either, with fennel, white wine, lemon butter, and fregola pasta. Finish the night off with a root-beer float made with their house-made ice cream and paired with a shot of locally distilled Copperworks whiskey. Yup, that was good.

Ballard

Sometimes You Gotta Go North for the Goods

THIS SLEEPY FISHING VILLAGE HAS EVOLVED INTO ONE OF THE most popular neighborhoods in Seattle. Originally home to Scandinavian fishermen, boat builders, and mill workers, to this day it is the largest fishing harbor in the Pacific Northwest. The action is condensed into two streets, Ballard Avenue and Market Street, that are lined with trendy restaurants, bakeries, quirky shops, bars, and craft breweries. With hip businesses opening on the daily, Ballard attracts all types of people: There's the early morning farmers' market and brunch crowd, late-night drunken debauchery crowd, post-work happy-hour crowd, and the local mamas who just want to get their nails did. Every summer, Ballard celebrates its fishing and Nordic roots with the annual SeafoodFest, a weekend featuring live music, endless amounts of traditional salmon barbecue, a skateboard competition (super random), and a beer garden. Beyond its really cute and walkable "downtown" area are urban gardens, playgrounds, Craftsman-style homes, and cringey high-rise condos. Activities include rock climbing at Stone Gardens or watching the salmon do their thing and boats pass by at the Ballard Locks. A five-minute drive from Ballard's hub is the numero uno place to catch the sunset, Golden Gardens Park. Grab a double scoop of Salt & Straw's crazy unique ice cream on the way and lounge out on the beach till it gets dark. This is a neighborhood totally worth exploring. Throw on your walking shoes, fill up on baked eggs and bennies at The Fat Hen, and get to it.

BALLARD CRAWL

1. **THE FAT HEN,** 1418 NW 70TH ST., SEATTLE, THEFATHENSEATTLE.COM, (206) 782-5422

2. **STONEBURNER,** 5214 BALLARD AVE. NW, SEATTLE, STONEBURNERSEATTLE.COM

3. **ASADERO PRIME,** 5405 LEARY AVE. NW, SEATTLE, ASADEROPRIME.COM, (206) 659-4499

4. **SAWYER,** 5309 22ND AVE NW SUITE A, SEATTLE, SAWYERSEATTLE.COM, (206) 420-7225

5. **SALT & STRAW,** 5420 BALLARD AVE. NW, SEATTLE, SALTANDSTRAW.COM, (206) 294-5581

6. **BITTERROOT BBQ,** 5239 BALLARD AVE. NW, SEATTLE, BITTERROOTBBQ .COM, (206) 588-1577

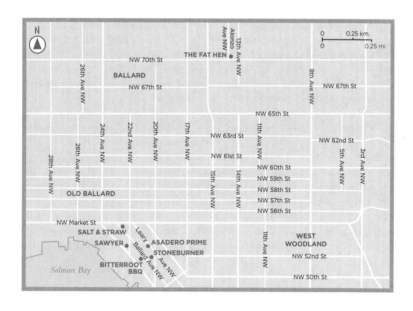

1

GETTING BAKED FOR BREAKFAST AT THE FAT HEN

The Fat Hen is a tiny neighborhood cafe serving breakfast and lunch daily. Cheerful morning vibes and always amazing egg dishes come out of this small, bright space—my go-to for taking out-of-towners. Weekend brunch is a suicide mission, as they seat 25 people max, so breakfast is the move, unless you enjoy spending your Saturday morning watching people through the window as they scarf down their picture-perfect Benedicts. Speaking of Benedicts, this is the very place I lost my Benedict virginity, and still to this day, theirs are my all-time favorite. Wild Alaskan salmon, Dungeness crab, prosciutto, pancetta, and Florentine Benedicts, all served with fingerling potatoes roasted in duck fat. The Egg Bakes are damn showstoppers. Tomato sauce so good I wanna sip on a mug of it all day. The Camicia comes studded with pockets of melty mozzarella, eggs, and fresh basil. The Alla Boscaiola with sausage and mushrooms. Each of the baked eggs arrives with a quarter of a chewy baguette for scooping up the last of the tomato sauce. Fun to share with your breakfast partner in crime is The Farmer, a rustic board with yummy house-made ricotta, pickled things, and salami. Also on their short menu are lattes, a random selection of morning pastries (omg, the cardamom twist), and fresh-squeezed grapefruit mimosas. You can order those at the counter and snack outside while you wait for a table. Don't make any big moves without taking a peek at the specials board highlighting seasonal items they have on hand, which are sure to be as tasty as the staple items. Arrive early and see for yourself why Seattle's obsessed with this damn cute establishment.

2 STEADILY BRUNCHIN' AT STONEBURNER

Finding a Ballard brunch spot that can accommodate your entire crew without the drama of waiting 30 minutes to be crammed into a tiny space is not an easy task. Literally all of Seattle wants to be in Ballard on Sunday, so if you're committing to finding a parking spot, your brunch better be good. Not to worry, chef and owner Jason Stoneburner consistently puts out some of the tastiest food and drink in the city. This spacious Ballard staple is located on the ground floor of the boutique Ballard Hotel. Its aesthetic is the perfect mix of classy and rustic, with oak paneling and repurposed vintage design elements from all over the globe. Large, expansive windows open up to charming Ballard Avenue, lighting up the restaurant. This is where you grub before boppin' around the Sunday farmers' market. Everything on the menu is solid, from the dutch baby to the pizzas.

You'll be swooning nonstop over the pizzas as they come out of the stone oven, so you better order one. Specifically the breakfast pizza with strips of bacon, potatoes, and eggs. You won't regret it, but you will regret not ordering one. Apparently pasta for brunch becomes appropriate with the addition of a flawlessly poached egg. Stoneburner's carbonara is still one of the highlights of my brunch career, with pancetta, cipollini onions, and a flurry of Parmesan. What brunch menu is complete without avocado toast? Stoneburner means business with their version of this hyped-up brunch item: a thick af slice of toast covered in a delightfully seasoned avocado mash and liquid-gold poached eggs. Right next to this Big Toast is two slices of bacon. That's how it's done around here. To continue our egg porn marathon, we have the crispy polenta cakes with poached eggs, smoky pimenton, and charred asparagus. To keep you busy while you wait for the arrival of these glorious food items are well-balanced brunch cocktails and freshly baked pastries.

3

PRIME TIME LUNCHING AT ASADERO PRIME

Carne asada for days — this is a carnivore's happy place. Once upon a time Asadero Prime was just a tiny hole-in-the-wall family-owned restaurant in Kent, but this Mexican steak house has recently moved north and quickly become Ballard's hottest spot to feast. The menu is inspired by the cuisine that, before the opening of Asadero, could only be found at Orozco family barbecues in northwestern Mexico. Beautiful cuts of high-quality beef skillfully grilled and smoked over mesquite charcoal. Chef-owner David Orozco sources the same meat that local high-end steak houses serve but sells it for about half the price. On just about every table is 16 ounces of their famed carne asada, simply grilled with sea salt and pepper, allowing the incredibly tender meat to flaunt its flavor. It comes with house-made flour

tortillas and is never complete without a visit to their salsa bar (it's amaze-balls). The guac is made to order, so it's extra fresh and fit to smother your carne asada. Served with whole, fried corn tortillas for breaking into pieces and scooping up the good stuff as you please. To go with all the carne asada, tacos, and tortas are epic appetizers: Tuetanos, a fire-roasted canoe of bone marrow, and Toritos, jalapeños stuffed with cream cheese and bacon. The menu is a pain in the ass to navigate, and trying to order can make your brain hurt. Play it safe; go with whatever your server recommends and take yourself on a meaty excursion. You may be here for the steak, but the beverage menu is also worthy of your attention. Horchata Alegre with coconut horchata and rum. A Mangojito and a Spicy Mezcalita will round out your meal. Asadero doesn't take reservations, so dinner is an absolute madhouse. Go for lunch and enjoy your carne asada in peace.

4

CRAVEABLE CREATIONS FOR DINNER AT SAWYER

If there's one thing I can say about Sawyer, it's that it has totally raised the bar for Seattle food. A new American tapas-style restaurant by chef Mitch Mayers in the heart of Ballard's booming restaurant scene. This mastermind is putting out smash-hit small and large plates, designed for family-style sharing. Banger after banger, Oxtails Nachos to S'mores Choco Tacos, this is the crave-worthy food you fantasize about late at night. It's creative and refined, like the stuff you'd find in a fine-dining restaurant, but casual enough so that you wouldn't think twice about hitting it multiple times a week. The Rotisserie Porchetta is my favorite dish on the menu. I'm declaring that the correct (and only) way to eat this is like a taco. Fork the tender pieces of porchetta and tuck them into the soft brioche-dough flatbread, then top it with the pickled veggies and assorted sauces. You won't know what hit ya. I'm on a quest to steal the recipe for the house salad dressing—it's that good.

The Cheesy Bread with pockets of pimento cheese is "shareable," but you should order two to avoid any awkward tension at the table. The menu goes on and on, and everything is worth ordering: Wood-Grilled Artichokes, Pork Belly Steam Buns, Rock Candy Spot Prawns with watermelon. For dessert, among others, are Dilly Bars with cookie-dough semifreddo and the most incredible Quatros Leches cake. They'll make your heart sing a happy song. Creative concoctions made from local spirits and fresh juices (cantaloupe and watermelon, yum) come from their beautiful full-service, floor-to-ceiling bar. You'll order drinks because of their names. The Nice

For What, with rhubarb, gin, and bubbles, would have Drake in tears.

The name Sawyer is a nod to the building's history as a sawmill. They've renovated but kept its original flooring and some of the woodwork from the 1920s, which adds to its coziness. The booths feel like little nooks, and there are long tables for group gatherings and an outdoor patio for weekend brunching. Get ready, Sawyer reels you in with its amazing food and keeps you coming back for more.

5
DESSERT AT SALT & STRAW CALLS FOR A DOUBLE SCOOP

Owners (and cousins) Kim and Tyler are pretty much ice-cream celebrities on the West Coast. Famed for their insanely creamy and out-of-the-box flavors, they've taken Portland and California by storm, and just recently this ice-cream tsunami has hit Seattle. They graced both Ballard and Capitol Hill with their new locations, scooping a mix of biggest hits, Seattle specials, and a monthly flavor series focused on seasonal ingredients. These addicting treats range from Beecher's Cheese with Peppercorn Toffee, Chocolate Gooey Brownie, and Strawberry Honey Balsamic with Black Pepper to gobs of tart cheesecake-like Ellenos yogurt swirled into matcha ice

cream. With dairy-free options like the Coconut Mint Chip Cupcake and the refreshing Rachel's Raspberry Ginger Beer, vegans can have fun, too. The sweet, sweet smell of their freshly made waffle cones travels down Ballard Avenue, and it only takes one inhale to get your attention. Prepare yourself for what seems to be a never-ending line, but once you finally reach the counter, endless amounts of samples will ensue. Even with the option to sample every flavor, anxiety can occur when you're trying to make a final decision. And for the extremely indecisive person who wants it all, they have a four-scoop tasting flight. Don't skip the selfie opportunity in front of the colorful, funky mural outside—it's important to flaunt your cone.

TIP

Grab a couple of pints out of the freezer and skip the entire line!

6 LATE NIGHT BBQ AT BITTERROOT

Every once in a while, I feel the need to dive face-first into a sea of barbecue, usually around 12:30 a.m. after hopping Ballard's stylish bars. I'd like to think I've earned this after releasing my inner Britney on the dance floor. Bitterroot BBQ serves their entire menu till 2 a.m. every damn day, and for that I am grateful. All the meats are smoked in-house and the portions are generous. Their late-night happy hour really is no joke. I'm talking $6 pulled pork sandwiches, $8 barbecue nachos, $3 cheddar grits, and $6 specialty cocktails, like their Creamed Old Fashioned. And with quite the impressive whiskey selection, I definitely recommend getting in the spirit with one of their whiskey flights. It's important you order the Smoked Jalapeño Hush Puppies; they're covered in a tangy mustard sauce and only $3 during happy hour. The mac and cheese is done in a "build your own" style so you can soup it up with toppings like collard greens, bacon, pulled pork, chili, and smoked jalapeños. Like I said, the portions are generous af; you'll for sure have enough to take home and eat on the couch the next day, since you'll most likely be a useless bum. The barbecue trays are a promising route: You pick from nine choices of meat, my go-to being the brisket or baby back ribs, although it's all juicy and wonderful. They want to show off the smoke of the meat so they serve it pre-sauce. The tables come equipped with three house-made barbecue sauces, letting you decide how

much you want to douse your meats. Then you pick two sides; as long as you order the Cast Iron Cornbread, we're cool. Damn, that honey butter soaks into the golden crust quite nicely. The space is Texas BBQ house meets Pottery Barn—you'll feel all cute and put together, while in reality you look a hot ass mess breaking down those ribs.

Downtown

Burgers + Ice-Cream Sundaes:
All a Girl Needs in Life

OH, DOWNTOWN SEATTLE, YOU'RE COMPLETELY MAD, but we love you. The busiest neighborhood in the city and home to one of the oldest farmers' markets in the United States, Pike Place Market, where, for reasons I will never understand, maniacs line up to go to the first ever Starbucks. (Pike Place has its very own chapter, we'll get to that later). Downtown is swarming with armies of both tourists and locals, with so much to do and so much to nosh on. Speaking of touristy things, there's plenty of them here, and they're not all so bad. The Great Wheel on Pier 57 is, well, a great way to check out the city. The wheel lights up all sorts of crazy colors; it's beautifully gimmicky and open till 12 a.m. on the weekend. Even if you're not an art aficionado, the Seattle Art Museum is worth the visit. They mix the exhibits up on the reg, so there's always something interesting to gaze upon with confusion. You'll find the usual corporate offices and shops, including Nordstrom's corporate office and flagship store (get ready to pop a tag or two). But the crème de la crème of Downtown are the restaurants. We are clearly blessed with awesome seafood, so this is where you wanna be to get down on some fresh salmon and king crab.

THE DOWNTOWN CRAWL

1. **MR. WEST,** 720 OLIVE WAY, SEATTLE, MRWESTCAFEBAR.COM, (206) 900-9378

2. **SIX SEVEN,** 2411 ALASKAN WAY, SEATTLE, EDGEWATERHOTEL.COM, (206) 269-4575

3. **PLACE PIGALLE,** 81 PIKE ST., SEATTLE, PLACEPIGALLE-SEATTLE.COM, (206) 624-1756

4. **HEARTWOOD PROVISIONS,** 1103 1ST AVE., SEATTLE, HEARTWOODSEA.COM, (206) 582-3505

5. **SHUG'S SODA FOUNTAIN,** 1525 1ST AVE., SEATTLE, SHUGSSODAFOUNTAIN .COM, (206) 602-6420

6. **LECŌSHO,** 89 UNIVERSITY ST., SEATTLE, LECOSHO.COM, (206) 623-2101

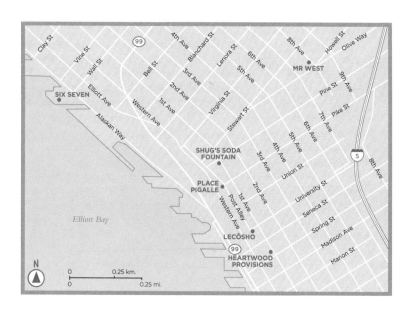

1 TREAT YOURSELF FOR BREAKFAST AT MR. WEST

We all have that guilty-pleasure cafe where we constantly justify spending 20-plus dollars on "breakfast." Or maybe that's just me, but I pick quality ass spots. Mr. West really has their shit together: stellar service, consistently great lattes, bomb cafe-style food, and a West Elm aesthetic. There are plants everywhere—they even have a selection of plants for you to adopt, surrounded by other things you don't need but will probably end up buying anyway. You have to pass by all of these cute items to get to the front counter, so it's not your fault. When you order, you'll play the "savory or sweet" game for a while. Their lavish toasts all sound so appealing. The avocado toast with mustard and curry sometimes causes me to neglect the almond butter toast with rhubarb compote, but it really just depends on my mood. Usually I would clown on someone if they ordered any sort of yogurt dish, but honestly, their apricot-rhubarb yogurt bowl with spiced almonds, honey, lime, and avocado (unexpectedly the best part) is my go-to. If you don't plan on staying, take a croissant breakfast sandwich to go—they bake the croissants fresh every morning. Unreal matcha lattes, thanks to one of the world's most important discoveries: oat milk. If you park your laptop at a table and work till the afternoon, you can get really committed by ordering one of their happy-hour cheese and meat boards.

2 ROCK STAR STATUS BRUNCH AT SIX SEVEN

Six Seven, inside the Edgewater Hotel, delivers a true Seattle experience with beautiful food. Literally on the edge of the Puget Sound, get ready to float away to brunch paradise. This place is legendary, it was built for the 1962 World's Fair, and the Beatles stayed here in 1964 during their first-ever world tour. Six Seven has hosted some of the most famous names in music: Pearl Jam, Led Zeppelin, the Rolling Stones, Ozzy Osbourne, KISS, Neil Young, Blondie. It's hard not to feel like a rock star just being there. But the brunch spread is the real headliner here. Kick things off like a boss with locally roasted Zoka coffee and a spicy Bloody Mary. The Dungeness crab Benedict and frittata are not to be missed. The Smoked Salmon Plate scores a 10 on both taste and appearance. This brunch mosaic features smoked salmon sourced down the street from the Pike Place Market, a round of caramelized Walla Walla onion, porcini cream cheese, and a chewy toasted bagel. The epic chicken and waffles is served as a stack of habanero waffles beside a mini frying basket filled with extremely well-breaded fried chicken and a tiny bottle of Tabasco (get your phone out for this one). The views are unbeatable, and so is the VIP treatment—you'll end up wanting to book a room.

3 LEISURELY LUNCHES AT PLACE PIGALLE

Hidden behind Pike Place Market's legendary fish throwers is my favorite place to lunch Downtown and where I demand you neglect your responsibilities, sip champagne, and grub on market-fresh Dungeness crab. To me, Place Pigalle is as Seattle as it gets. The funny thing is that most locals don't even know this delicious spot exists. It's possible you'll score a window seat with an unreal view of Elliot Bay, the Olympic Mountains, and the Great Wheel. The patio seats aren't too shabby either, and calling ahead to ensure you grab one isn't a bad idea. The menu is a mix of modern and traditional French cuisine, obviously incorporating the bounty of market goodies. Your server will fill you in on the rotating seasonals, but here to stay is the Bitter Greens and Beans, simply amazing sautéed greens and cannellini beans dressed in lots of lemon, garlic, and Parmesan. It's great for off-setting all of the gruyère cheese from the French onion soup. Their takes on duck confit and croque madame are both very solid. And, yes, the menu is loaded with oysters, mussels, and other salty sea creatures for you seafood junkies. If there was a time to try escargot, it is now. It arrives doused in tarragon butter, garlic, and shallots—add rosé for maximum pleasure. If you're taking the time to lunch here, you probably have nowhere else to be, so why not crack into a perfectly torched crème brûlée to finish off this flawless outing?

4 MIND-BLOWING DINNER PAIRINGS AT HEARTWOOD PROVISIONS

Everything about drink pairings has always seemed so snobby and bogus to me. I'm the type of girl who prefers to eat her calories, anyway. But Heartwood Provisions has converted me into a drink-pairing believer. Only beverage director Amanda Reed's cocktails could make chef Varin Keokitvon's food taste better than it already does. The menu features various innovative dishes, some with the pairing options listed below. You must explore these; each concoction enhances and completes the flavors of its paired menu item. What they got going on here is a seemingly effortless marriage between kitchen and bar. They've even paired up their charcuterie boards. Cheese, meat and alcohol: things we need to survive. Paired or not, every single thing on the menu is 10/10 would recommend. Their brussel sprouts and fries are fried in tallow, which is essentially beef fat. Who wouldn't be down with that? A grilled pork chop nearly the size of a newborn is served with a skillet of gruyère potatoes. The first bite will have your eyes rolling back in your head. Same goes for the stack of spicy, chewy yet tender Wagyu Beef Jerky. This should be on every menu, and if they're as smart as I think they are, they'd package and sell this crack. The yellowtail dish with avocado and grapefruit is so pretty you'll probably freak out. I

could list their entire menu, because it's all worthy of a moment, but I won't. Just promise me you'll order the Pork Shoulder Poutine off the bar menu and the Khaleesi's Reign cocktail with pear-infused vodka, BroVo vermouth, chamomile, lemon, and sparkling wine—so good it deserves the Iron Throne. You can slap yourself if you don't finish off the meal with the Smoked Caramel Panna Cotta—it's unforgettable.

5

NOSTALGIC TREATS AT SHUG'S SODA FOUNTAIN

Downtown was seriously lacking in dessert options, but then Shug's, aka a sweet fiend's fantasy, came to our rescue. Owners Colleen and Paul are pushing all of your nostalgic buttons with their classic yet modern soda fountain and ice-cream parlor, a light, whimsical space with marble countertops, white stools, and sweet pops of pastel. They've restored a 1930s soda fountain, in which they're cranking out soda water and mixing it with their house-made syrups. Hitting you with a little Throwback Thursday is their version of a retro favorite, the Creamsicle, which they call the Shugsicle. The overflowing bubbles will bring out your inner, giddy 10-year-old. More age appropriate is the section of their menu dedicated to boozy cocktails. I frequent the Prosecco Float; it makes me feel extra boujee. It comes in the most adorable bird-bath prosecco-filled glass with peach sorbet. You could totally just order a scoop of one of their 15 flavor options, locally sourced from Lopez Island Creamery, and pimp it out with warm apple compote, sprinkles, and scratch-made syrups. Or you can let Shug's play dress-up with one of their ridiculously bomb sundaes. The S'more sundae gets a lot of attention, and she deserves it: house-made marshmallows and graham crackers roasted tableside with a hand torch, atop of a hot fudge-coated (vintage) glass with vanilla ice cream. The menu seems endless, listing off a wide range of treats: affogatos, hot chocolates, shakes, egg creams, and more. Whatever you end up diving into will be pure magic.

TIP

The Dixie Split is a "secret menu" item that will rock your world. It's basically a banana split but 20 times better thanks to the brûléed bananas and Shug's caramel sauce voodoo.

6 LET'S DO LATE NIGHT AT LECŌSHO

Halfway down the Harbor Steps is an outstanding restaurant named Lecōsho. European-influenced dishes using ingredients the Northwest does best: wild mushrooms, cheese, seafood, and locally and sustainably sourced meats. Everything is house-made, including their charcuterie, sausage, and

pasta. You won't find a place with better food or a better atmosphere that stays open this late downtown. The dark, candlelit space is great for masking how ridiculous you'll look slurping down the wild boar and beef Bolognese. Lecōsho does everything right, but it's about time they're crowned for best burger in Seattle. This burger starts with a half pound of pink and juicy Painted Hills beef, pickled red onions, spicy aioli, and Beecher's Flagship cheddar

TIP

Their quaint patio is the perfect happy-hour hangout, especially with $5 wine pours.

inside a grilled ciabatta bun. Modest, clean, nothing crazy. Thankfully, it's available on both their lunch and late-night menus. But I can assure you it's best enjoyed under the influence of Mary Jane and with added bacon. Also gracing the late-night menu is a pork belly banh mi that's as good as it sounds, if not better. Short ribs are a must. Cocktails are worth every penny and made by bartenders who actually know what they're doing. You'll receive nothing but incredible service, food, and drink. And even if you're not Downtown, this burger is worth the Lyft and trek down the Harbor Steps. This Seattle industry and local favorite is how you end your night on a sophisticated note.

Belltown

Boujee Cocktails Will Put You on Tapa the World

BELLTOWN IS DOWNTOWN'S UNDERRATED NEXT-DOOR neighbor. Covered in trendy high-rise apartments and condos with stunning views of the Puget Sound and the Olympic Mountains. The old storefronts have been converted into top-notch bars and restaurants, making this a night-out destination. You could barhop this neighborhood seven nights in a row and still not hit all of its watering holes. But, wherever your night takes you, it must end with multiple rolls of sushi at Umi and start with a table full of tapas at Pintxo. Moviegoers adore Belltown's Cinerama—a vintage panoramic theater with a ton of history, a starry ceiling, authentic costumes, and hit-movie premieres. The best part, really, is the chocolate popcorn, though. The Crocodile lives on 2nd and has stolen the hearts of many. It's a small music venue where big-name bands, including Nirvana, Pearl Jam, and the Beastie Boys, have jammed out. Today, its calendar lists the names of both local and international up-and-coming artists, many recognizable. I always peep the calendar in case someone I dig is coming to town. On the northern edge of Belltown is Sculpture Park, tons of grass for lying and paths for walking beside a restored beach, plus some bizarre "contemporary" art pieces. Schlep your Pike Place goodies here, because this is some fantastic picnic territory.

THE BELLTOWN CRAWL

1. **BISCUIT BITCH,** 1711, 2303 3rd Ave., Seattle, biscuitbitch.com, (206) 728-2219

2. **TILIKUM PLACE CAFÉ,** 407 CEDAR ST., SEATTLE, TILIKUMPLACECAFE.COM, (206) 282-4830

3. **PINTXO,** 2219 4TH AVE., SEATTLE, PINTXOSEATTLE.COM, (206) 441-4042

4. **LOCAL 360,** 2234 1ST AVE., SEATTLE, LOCAL360.ORG, (206) 441-9360

5. **UMI,** 2230 1ST AVE., SEATTLE, UMISAKEHOUSE.COM, (206) 374-8717

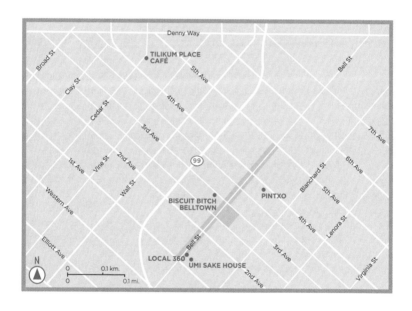

1 A BITCHIN' BREAKFAST AT BISCUIT BITCH

Is it the name? Is it the biscuits? Is it the bitchin' Southern hospitality? It's just about everything and more. When owner and head bitch Kim Spice opened this biscuit palace, she vowed that no customer would ever feel the very real "Seattle freeze," and she's keeping that promise. As soon as you enter, your ears will be greeted by raunchy music (que "Move Bitch" by Ludacris) and a "What up bitches?" Brace yourself—you'll say bitch at least five times, as each biscuit is its own kind of bitch. I'm sure you can resonate with the Hot Mess Bitch—a warm biscuit smothered in country sausage or shiitake mushroom gravy, eggs, cheesy garlic grits, a grilled Louisiana hot link, and jalapeños—even more so on a Sunday morning at 9 a.m. The Bitchwitch is simply a must-get, a biscuit sammy with their spicy bitchin' sauce, sausage, lots of cheese, and an egg. The sweetest of them all is the Nutty Bitch, with bananas, Nutella, and an excessive amount of whip . . . I'm not mad about it. If you're into the Easy Bitch, your biscuit will arrive with gravy and two over-easy eggs. The portions are huge; it's total madness. Like one of these biscuits could very well be your breakfast, lunch, and midafternoon snack. They'll prepare you for hibernation or put you straight into a food coma. Get there before 2 p.m., because this sassy "trailer park to table" establishment serves breakfast and breakfast only. The Belltown location is about twice as big as the original location near Pike Place Market, making lines move faster and seating less of a . . . bitch.

2

DUTCH BABY DREAMIN'
AT TILIKUM PLACE CAFÉ

This dutch baby hot spot is typically recommended for brunch, but if you want to save yourself an hour, you'll make this a lunch outing. The only thing you'll miss out on is the Benedict, but you didn't come for that. You came for chef-owner Ba Culbert's unique take on dutch babies—a rustic pancake/crepe/popover hybrid in a personal-size cast-iron skillet. The hype is real, people. The inside is quiche-like—light and fluffy with a crispy outside. You'll choose from three options: classic, sweet, or savory. These dutch babies change with the season, just like the rest of the short and carefully designed menu. The sweet is freaking fantastic with a large handful of blueberries, lemon, and ricotta. Savory is just as divine, with chorizo, queso fresco (which makes for a cheesy crust), and Fresno chiles. Both come with a side of maple syrup, so make sure to give that baby a golden shower — it's worth every calorie. If you're hangry and eager for these carb bombs, order them immediately, as they can take up to 25 minutes to make. Get that portrait mode ready— the heaps of natural light make for a flawless dutch baby glamour shot. These dutch babies slay hard but don't sleep on Tilikum's baked eggs. They're some of the best around. The not-your-typical soup-and-sandwich combo of French onion and a tofu banh mi is up there, too. Tucked away on Cedar Street, this cozy European-inspired cafe is a Seattle signature. With its charming details, from exposed brick to the tiny shortbread cookies served alongside your French press coffee, you'll feel so welcome you'll never want to leave. It's just a short walk from the Space Needle, so if you plan on checking that landmark out, you must make a delicious detour here. Pssstt . . . reservations really never hurt.

3

PINTXO IS MY TAPA DINNER

Pintxo, Pintxo, Pintxo. A Belltown favorite whipping up bomb tapas for the masses. Modern takes on traditional dishes from various culinary regions of Spain, best enjoyed with your main squeezes and a liter of sangria. Pintxo's looks have beauty-pageant status, winning Seattle's most beautiful restaurant in 2017. There's a massive stained-glass installation above the bar, a major wow factor and taste of classic Spanish architecture. Yes, the restaurant is drop-dead gorgeous, but you're here to eat and drink it all. First step, order the paella—it takes about 30 minutes to cook, and you'll be glad you got a jump on this skillet of seafoody-rice bliss. Next, order the bacon-wrapped dates. These are stuffed with goat cheese, and the bacon is crisped and caramelized by the juice of the date. You've probably had your fair share of restaurant octopus, but this one is slow braised in serrano-ham broth—so tender, so heavenly. Patatas Bravas (seriously addictive fried potatoes), shishito peppers, pork empanadas, steak skewers, and Ibérico ham that melts in your mouth—the deal here is to order it all. Fill your table with delicious small plates and work on them till the paella arrives. Pintxo is also

known for their "gins and tins," a variety of imported tinned seafood items paired with cardamom-speckled gin and tonic–filled goblets. Inside these cute tins are the most delightful mussels, sardines, and clams dressed with olive oil and herbs and served with bread. This is a prime spot to nosh on delicious tapas with friends or that cutie you've been nonstop texting. A few glasses of Spanish wine and a plate of Basque sausages might teleport you both to Barcelona.

4

AFTER DINNER WE HAVE DESSERT AT LOCAL 360

Local 360 has a pretty dang cool mission statement: They're focused on sustainability and local sourcing, and almost everything served is made using ingredients falling within 360 miles of the restaurant. But no concept of theirs tops their genius sweets. I'm talking PB&J Bon Bons that literally explode warm peanut-butter goo in your mouth. They come with a mini glass "shooter" of milk, which will complete your entire life. Fruit Crisps that change with the season, my favorite being the strawberry-rhubarb, hot and crumbly with a scoop of Lopez Island vanilla ice cream. You'll get so much pleasure cracking into the caramelized top of the crème brûlée, breaking into its creamy, vanilla bean–speckled insides. Drink your sugar with one of the two options of organic hot cocoa, one spicy, both rich and delicious. And why not booze it up with one of their dessert cocktails? The Hazelnut Coffee packs a buzz with Crater Lake Hazelnut vodka, Blue Star coffee, and amaretto whip. A list of dessert wines, whiskey, and cheeses exists for the weirdos born without a sweet tooth. The space has a cozy farmhouse feel to it, tall booths and long tables made of recycled wood and a little street-side patio that you can chill on while living the sweet life. And if you like chicken and waffles, you should stop by for weekend brunch.

5

SATISFY YOUR LATE NIGHT SUSHI CRAVING AT UMI

When it comes to sushi, there are plenty of places in Seattle that know what they're doing. We all have our go-to, and mine is Umi Sake House. On 1st Avenue, Umi's unassuming entry leads you into a gorgeous Japanese teahouse. From front to back are different rooms, each offering a totally different vibe. Sip endless amounts of sake while sitting on tatami mats in the private dining room, become friends with the chef at the wooden sushi bar, or vibe out in the garden room with tropical plants, lanterns, and skylights. The menu is stacked with pages and pages of sashimi, specialty rolls, and 60-plus bottles of imported Japanese sake. It's best to tackle it family style; order a bunch of appetizers and rolls, share them, then attempt to single out a favorite. Really, go for whatever rolls sound good—they're all inventive

and uniquely delicious. The 206 Roll has got it all going on—sweet snow crab legs, cucumber, avocado, and cream cheese topped with spicy tuna, tobiko, green onions, spicy ponzu, and wasabi aioli. The Mango Tango roll packs a fruity flare, bright with tuna, mango, cilantro, and bell peppers. The Rainbow Tartare, a vibrant tower of tuna, yellowtail, salmon, shrimp, avocados, and warm rice topped with the yummiest of sauces, looks so good that you'll get excited and swipe right twice. If settling on a few items is

TIP

The late-night happy hour is reason enough to visit: half off the chirashi bowl, $6 tempura platter, and discounted rolls and sake pours.

too daunting, I advise you to order the Omakase Board (chef's selection of sushi and sashimi) as it's a fantastic way to experience all things Umi and the Northwest's freshest seafood. Also on the menu are wonderful soups, noodle bowls, and tempura that I love dearly. And I'm stoked to say that you can find my favorite cocktail here, the Lychee Lemonade: vanilla vodka, Giffard lychee liqueur, fresh lemon juice, cranberry juice, and a lychee fruit. Umi stays open till 2a.m. with 12 a.m. being the last call for food orders. This is where you wanna be before or after a night out in Belltown.

West Seattle

Spam Musubi on the Beach = Perfection

WEST SEATTLE FEELS LIKE ITS OWN LITTLE CITY. This residential area has a beach-town charm, laid-back vibe, growing restaurant scene, and a strong sense of community. Most people travel across the West Seattle Bridge to set up camp at Alki. This beach strip is probably the No. 1 Seattle destination on a summer day. If you're not much of a beached whale, there's still a ton to do: play beach volleyball, barbecue and roast s'mores at one of the many firepits, kayak, bike, paddleboard, or grab that flawless Seattle skyline shot. And there's no shortage of grub along this beach front, local favorite being Marination Ma Kai for tacos and katsu sammies. The Junction is considered the downtown of West Seattle and also has a lot to offer—consignment stores, coffeehouses, massive scoops of ice cream at the OG Husky Deli, and vinyl digging at Easy Street Records and Cafe. We Seattleites love a good farmer's market, and West Seattle's can hang with the best of them. Every Sunday from 10 a.m. to 2 p.m. the streets of The Junction are flooded with a variety of the finest local things: fresh produce, cheeses, meats, baked goods, flowers, kombucha, beer/wine/cider, and awesome food trucks. This neighborhood is all about supporting local—most of what you'll find here is unique to West Seattle (aka very few chain establishments), which is pretty refreshing. Seattleites like to act as if West Seattle is a faraway land. It's definitely a bit out of the way, but it's worth the drive.

THE WEST SEATTLE CRAWL

1. **ARTHUR'S,** 2311 CALIFORNIA AVE. SW, SEATTLE, ARTHURSSEATTLE.COM, (206) 829-8235

2. **EASY STREET RECORDS AND CAFE,** 4559 CALIFORNIA AVE. SW, SEATTLE, EASYSTREETONLINE.COM/CAFE, (206) 938-3279

3. **MARINATION MA KAI,** 1660 HARBOR AVE. SW, SEATTLE, MARINATIONMOBILE.COM, (206) 328-8226

4. **RACCOLTO,** 4147 CALIFORNIA AVE. SW, SEATTLE, RACCOLTOSEATTLE.COM, (206) 397-3775

5. **HUSKY DELI,** 4721 CALIFORNIA AVE .SW, SEATTLE, HUSKYDELI.COM, (206) 937-2810

6. **THE MATADOR,** 4546 CALIFORNIA AVE. SW, SEATTLE, MATADORRESTAURANTS.COM, (206) 932-9988

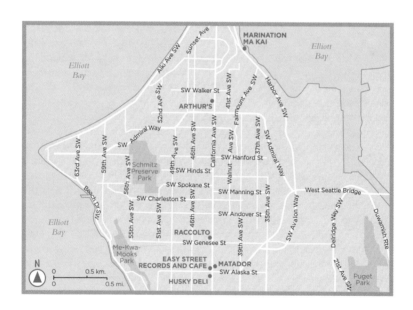

1

BREAKFAST DOWN UNDER AT ARTHUR'S

Seattle would truly benefit from an Arthur's in every hood. This super-chic Australian-inspired cafe serves breakfast all day, with a majority of the dishes being basically healthy and light. I was honestly hesitant about including this spot simply because I love the fact that I can always get a table and really don't want that to change. So only tell your most favorite person about Arthur's, please. It's totally trendy with succulents all over the walls, plants everywhere, and that white subway tile that's in the dream kitchen you'll probably never have. This is where you take your fashion blogger best friend who cares how cute a place is. Besides, it would be insanely rude to keep her away from the yummiest pancakes in the entire universe. These blueberry ricotta buttermilk pancakes result in continuous mouthgasms. I'm offering a money-back guarantee on this one, people. An egg dish that sits on top of pumpkin puree is bizarre but amazing at the same time. Apparently this is the norm in Australia, and I'm down with it. It's called the Forager's Rosti, and it also comes with wild mushrooms, garlic, fresh herbs, spinach, toasted walnuts, and crispy sage—baller. You could probably assume that they have an avocado toast to match their perfect aesthetic (they do, and it's damn good). There's a chia seed pudding with fresh fruit, in case you're constipated but also wanting something delicious. The Arthur's Breakfast Bowl comes with kale, root veggies, quinoa, a fat pork sausage, pickled bell peppers, vintage white cheddar, and a fried egg. Get on it, mate. You know what would make this Instagram-ready tablescape shot complete? An almond-milk latte. They have a full-service espresso machine, so go wild. If this is what the cafes in Melbourne are like, I'm purchasing a one-way ticket ASAP. P.S. There's a patio out front in case you plan on diving headfirst into a sea of bottomless mimosas.

2

BUST A MOVE DURING BRUNCH AT EASY STREET

Easy Street Records and Cafe is where the best of both worlds meet: music and food. Part record store and part diner, you'll work up an appetite sifting through boxes of vinyls and CDs. If you're on a mission to persuade your hip cousin to move to Seattle, you should bring them here. This place is grunge kingdom and just oozes cool. You can expect a wait during the weekend, but with about a zillion things to look at, you'll forget you even put your name down. There's a rad coffee bar in the middle, with vintage diner-esque stools. The place is covered in posters and artwork of bands that rep the area, so you'll likely find yourself in a deeply caffeinated episode of nostalgia. Don't be quick to judge the cafe by its gritty interior; food is A-plus, prices are low, and a majority of the menu is dedicated to music legends. A steak and eggs Johnny Cash special, Dolly Parton pancake stack with bacon and eggs your way. The huevos rancheros will have you dancing to whatever tunes they're spinning.

Make sure you have a cup of water nearby if you order the Horton Heat Hash; a hott hodgepodge of corned beef, bacon, onions, peppers, hash browns, and secret spices. That son of a b will sneak up on you. There's plenty of vegetarian options like the Beck omelet with veggie bacon and the Soundgarden burger. If you're not starving to death but need a little

fuel for record browsing, holler at the queen bitch Lil' Kim—one piece of french toast, bacon, and an egg. Sometimes one piece of french toast just isn't gonna cut it, and that's why they hook you up with two when you order the Frances Farmer French Toast. Spend the extra $3 on a Mudhoney latte with chocolate and honey; it will have you on one. The only thing missing from this true Seattle landmark is an Eddie Vedder sighting.

The two locations have hosted a total of 500 live in-house performances, including big-name artists like Lou Reed, Lana Del Rey, Kings of Leon, and Northwest-grown artists like the Shins, Band of Horses, and the Blue Scholars.

3 HAWAIIAN LUNCH VIBES AT MARINATION MA KAI 📷

Aloha, bitches! Little did you know Hawaiian street food was one of the Seattle eats you were destined to consume. In 2009, Marination started as a food truck hustle, where owners Kamala and Roz graced us with their unique Korean-Hawaiian fusion cuisine, and now they've opened up spots in Capitol Hill, South Lake Union, and West Seattle. There's something oh so special about their Ma Kai location, with literally the best view of all of Seattle and an extended menu; you'll never want to give up your patio seat. There's a bar where you can order boozy shave ice and some of the best local brews. With prices and flavors like these, I recommend going with a solid group and ordering a couple of everything on the menu. The Pork Katsu Sandwich has levels to it—juicy pork cutlet with the crunch factor we're all looking for in breading, cabbage slaw, and a slew of sweet yet sour sauces all held together by a Macrina Bakery ciabatta bun. All of the tacos and sliders are legit; $3 apiece and topped with slaw and Nunya sauce. Or get the fish-and-chips, which always tastes ten times better scarfed down seaside. I strongly suggest going with their kalua pork, quite dreamy packed in the sweet Hawaiian slider buns. Even if you're not a Spam person, order the Spam stuff. Don't be intimidated by the line out the door—it moves fast and the food comes out even faster. If you're feeling adventurous, you can catch the water taxi from Downtown Seattle and you'll dock 10 feet away from this waterfront hangout.

4

DINNER NOODS AT RACCOLTO

The number of top of the line pasta spots is increasing in Seattle, but Raccolto has my heart. There are many reasons why I commit carbocide here. To name a few: surprisingly inexpensive and fresh house-made pastas, seafood sourced from their very own seafood market, seasonally changing vegetable dishes, and boss status Italian wines. Everything is presented simply, which mirrors the clean space. It's a small bi-level restaurant with floor-to-ceiling windows that open during the warmer days, industrial lighting, and an open kitchen with counter seating. The small, yet adorable upstairs makes for an intimate setting, great for a dinner party or special celebration.

I love that Raccolto has a total neighborhood feel; you can tell most of the diners are regulars. And since West Seattle rolls at a slower pace, your dinner experience will feel that much more chill. For crunchy, leafy greens that will make your insides happy, go for the the Gem Lettuce salad, lemony goodness topped with massive croutons and a mountain of ricotta salata. Also great is the Dungeness crab tossed with thinly cut apples, fennel, and snap peas. I'm almost positive the kitchen crew frantically picks the ingredients seconds before plating, that's how bright and refreshing these salads are. One of their most popular bites features a generous amount of smoked salmon, capers, and pickled shallots atop grilled Macrina bread. It's sort of like fancy lox.

The fresh seafood saga continues with albacore crudo, oysters with house horseradish, and whatever rotating sea creature is listed under "proteins." They occasionally switch up their pasta offerings, but a few stick around. It can be exceptionally difficult to decide which ones to order, but there are no right or wrongs—one with red sauce and one with white is usually my strategy. I could slurp those bucatini noodles for hours. Always al dente tagliatelle with a porcini ragù, Fresno chili, and crème fraîche. Strozzapreti with a Bolognese so good it will make your heart skip a beat. If I were a trust-fund baby, traveling across the West Seattle Bridge for plates of angelic pasta would be a nightly thing.

5 ICE-CREAM THERAPY AT HUSKY DELI

Husky Deli is conclusive evidence as to why ice cream is the best thing on earth: It's dependable, loyal, and the answer to any and every problem. Established in 1932, this family-run deli continues to churn out this creamy elixir of life. The staff is super friendly and likely a member of the Miller family. They have over 20-something flavors in the case, making it hard to single out just one (or two). There are three Oreo-centric flavors in the mix, so clearly they've got their heads on straight. Coffee Oreo is a must, alone or paired with a scoop of banana. And if you see horchata in the case, do not hesitate. The line-up is full of winners: chocolate fudge brownie, blackberry cheesecake, Thin Mint, lemon custard . . . all of which they will make into a shake, if that's your calling. Compared to the other frozen treat shops in Seattle, the scoops here are freakin' huge. Which obviously I'm not complaining about; I'm not one of those calorie-counting maniacs who asks for smaller scoops. Oh, and waffle cones are made fresh in-store, which explains that intoxicating aroma. Did I mention this ice cream is mad cheap? Yeah, a quart is only $9 (seems like a solid investment to me). This is also a place for killer sandwiches, classic candy in bulk, craft beverages, and other munchies. There are a few vintage stools and tables you can sit at and enjoy whatever goods you end up swooping. The deli looks as if it hasn't been remodeled for at least 60 years, making you feel like you're in a small town. I'm pretty sure West Seattle would start a riot if Husky Deli were to close, and I'd happily join in.

6 LATE-NIGHT NACHO BINGE AT THE MATADOR

I love getting sloppy, and by that I mean I love face-planting into a colossal plate of $5 nachos at 12 a.m. You would think I'm about to win a free T-shirt and get my photo on the wall. The Matador's late-night menu really does slay: bomb ass Tex-Mex eats ranging from $2 to $6, and they're available till 1 a.m. Like okay, we'll take one of everything and see you again tomorrow night. The bar is locked and loaded with over 100 types of tequila—seems a bit excessive, but I guess it's cool to have the Northwest's largest selection of tequila. Basically what I'm trying to say is, your margarita is going to be really good. The food is where things start to get a little out of hand. When the stuffed jalapeños hit the table, it's a fight to the death. These spicy little muchachos are filled with goat cheese and wrapped with hickory-smoked bacon. Watch out, the habanero shrimp have that fire-lingering heat. Tally up the street tacos, it's one for $2, three for $5, or five for $8. I'm gonna

make a special shout-out to the fried pork belly tacos; they go above and beyond. Remember, you're here for the really cheap, really good nachos. If your table doesn't have at least one order on it you're failing at life. The ambiance is mad casual and sexy with candles everywhere and a cool fire-pit to lounge around. On most nights you'll be able to snag a table without waiting; like I said, West Seattle is low-key like that. You'll leave relaxed, full, and buzzed—sounds like an ideal situation to me. They also have a Ballard location, so you can get down on some $5 nachos there as well.

Bonus Crawl!

Seattle's Best Pizza
Because Pizza Is Life

Pizza acts as an emotional support for many, but especially for us Seattle-ites. While living in potentially the most gloomy city ever, we are used to leaning on life's simple pleasures to keep the seasonal depression at bay. Luckily, Seattle, a smorgasbord of cuisines, has access to just about every type of pizza you could imagine: Neapolitan, New Jersey, Chicago deep-dish . . . and that just goes to say, round or square, we don't care. Just give us our za and make it good. Here are a few of the many pie spots in Seattle that really stand out.

THE PIZZA CRAWL

1. **THE MASONRY**, 730 N 34TH ST., SEATTLE, THEMASONRYSEATTLE.COM, (206) 557-4907
2. **VON'S 1000 SPIRITS**, 1225 1ST AVE., SEATTLE, VONS1000SPIRITS.COM, (206) 621-8667
3. **PATXI'S PIZZA**, 5323 BALLARD AVE. NW, SEATTLE, PATXISPIZZA.COM, (206) 946-1512
4. **MIOPOSTO**, 3426 NE 55TH ST., SEATTLE, MIOPOSTOPIZZA.COM, (206) 582-1899
5. **DINO'S TOMATO PIE**, 1524 E. OLIVE WAY, SEATTLE, DINOSTOMATOPIE.COM, (206) 403-1742
6. **BAR DEL CORSO**, 3057 BEACON AVE. S, SEATTLE, BARDELCORSO.COM, (206) 395-2069

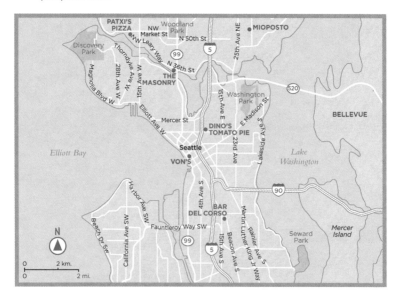

1

MICROBREWS & MARGZAS AT THE MASONRY

The Masonry didn't just land a spot on this epic pizza list because of its perfect Neapolitan pizza; its impressive list of craft beers and stupidly delicious meatballs also helped secure it a spot. Because pizza and beer go together like Seattleites and Birkenstocks. If you're sitting inside, you can watch homie cranking pizzas out of the wood-fired oven like a madman. Their Margherita pizza is easily my fav marg in the city, with a heaven-sent tomato sauce and just the right amount of mozz. Its small-medium size and fresh ingredients make taking the whole thing down by yourself not embarrassing. The crust is chewy and fluffy with those giant charred doughy bubbles that are hard not to gawk at. The aforementioned meatballs are euphoric and served with warm focaccia bread. You should dip your pizza crust into the leftover meatball sauce once you run out of focaccia. I gotta thing for their Caesar salad, and the cream-based mushroom pizza keeps me coming back for more. With long wooden tables and a turntable spinning the cuts, The Masonry is choice for a group outing. Patio seating is also a go, with a ton more tables covered by hot pink umbrellas (if you're walking around Fremont and see these, then you know you're in the right place). A super relaxed atmosphere to drink microbrews, munch on meatballs, and laugh about the stupid shit Karen said during the meeting today.

2 VON'S SOURDOUGH PIZZA WILL CHANGE YOUR LIFE

There's nothing quite like a Von's pizza, because they're the only ones smart enough to make sourdough za. They've been rocking with the same sourdough starter for 60-plus years, which makes the dough tangy and wonderful. It has a chew to it like no other; it's a major game changer. And because they've mastered this sourdough, they're totally running with it; sourdough mac and cheese, burgers, and sandwiches—do you sense a theme here? All of these carby things are great, but the boat-shaped, almond-wood-fired pizza is a major heartthrob. This being a scratch kitchen, every single ingredient is sourced carefully, so each topping serves its purpose. Pepperoni from Olympia Provisions, a little bit spicy and will make every other pepperoni seem "blah." The Walla Walla Onion Chutney Pizza is a bit sweeter than the norm, but the goat cheese, pesto, and prosciutto balance it all out. It's almost impossible to pick a favorite until the Cuban pork avocado za made an appearance. I'm literally salivating just typing about it: carefully topped with 12-hour braised pork shoulder, pickled onion, and Reggiano all drizzled with a zesty avocado salsa. These guys are well-known for their spun-sugar cocktails. I hate that I love The Skinny Bitch; it's made with their house vodka, fresh grapefruit and cranberry juices, plus a fluff of cotton candy that's melted tableside (make sure to capture the pour on video). I can shamelessly consume two or more of these in a sitting.

3

THINGS ARE GETTING DEEP AT PATXI'S PIZZA

I stopped planning my next trip to Chicago the moment Patxi's set up shop in Ballard. Just like the authentic stuff, Patxi's deep-dish consists of layers of cheese and toppings covered in tomato sauce, all snug inside a thick crust. The ample amount of melty mozzarella requires a fork 'n' knife and makes for an insane cheese pull. You can build your own pie, choosing from over 20 different toppings and four different types of cheese (including vegan cheese), or go for one of their pie creations. On the not-so-conventional side is the BBQ Chicken pie stuffed with smoked bacon and finished with a cilantro and jalapeño shower. Then there's the classic pies, like the Special with garlic-fennel sausage, fresh mushrooms, green peppers, and onions, and the Spinach Pesto with heaps of fresh spinach and a garlicky pesto sauce. This should always be a team effort, as taking down one of these pizzas alone could probably sedate a horse. It takes no less than 30 minutes for the deep-dish pies to bake, so make sure to put your order in ASAP. Nosh on delicious things like burrata bruschetta with pesto and a chopped salad while the cheesy magic is happening. And visit during happy hour for $3 off beer, wine, and

cocktails and $5 personal pizzas. Cozy, casual, and kid friendly, Patxi's has become a neighborhood staple in Ballard. The servers are easygoing and can somehow put up with my entire zoo of a family. I'd say that alone is deserving of a five-star review.

4

PIZZA FOR BREAKFAST AT MIOPOSTO

You're a grown-ass tax-paying adult who can eat whatever the hell you want, so if pizza for breakfast sounds good, head to one of Mioposto's four locations and get busy. The coziest of neighborhood pizzerias, meaning no matter what time of day or how big your group, you'll get seated, be treated like fam, and eat pizza until your vision gets blurry. Their brunch game is a little bit underrated and a whole lot bomb. The Bacon & Egg Breakfast Pizza is good just about any time of the day, but it's especially satisfying the morning after abusing your body at the bars. The house-made tutto calabria sauce gives it some heat, the pancetta gives it zing, seasoned bread crumbs for some crunch, and the sunny-side up eggs make it a work of art. This pizza is an absolute must order. If you're lunch-ing or dinner-ing, a couple of small plates should be on the table. There's an entire sliced tomato on their caprese salad, topped with fragrant basil, fresh mozzarella, and chunks of sea salt. Simple and excellent. A beautiful antipasti board with handfuls of goat cheese, olive tapenade, agrodolce, roasted and marinated eggplant, prosciutto, and arugula with Mio baked bread. The Prosciutto e Arugula is a pizza disguised as a salad—yes, please. The almighty Zucca Balsamica is topped with just about everything they have on hand: olive oil, mozzarella, roasted butternut squash, pancetta, caramelized onions, garlic, rosemary, goat cheese, red pepper flakes, and a balsamic reduction. If this pizza sounds

obnoxiously over the top, think again. Mioposto does a kick-ass job honor-
ing the simplicity and authenticity of traditional Neapolitan pizzerias, using
as many domestically sourced ingredients as possible and cooking them
with only the heat from the open-fire wood oven. The name means "my
place" in Italian, and this really is my place for pizza at any time of the day.

5

DINO'S TOMATO PIE LIKES 'EM THICK

Dino's Tomato Pie on Capitol Hill serves pizza round and square, delicious and binge-worthy. This place was dreamed up and inspired by the New Jersey pizzerias that owner Brandon Pettit frequented growing up. It's got that true old-school pizza joint vibe with red plastic water cups, paper plates, family photos on the wall, big cozy booths, and good-ass, no-fuss pizza. It's totally reminiscent of the pizza place I went to as a kid for my soccer team parties—#lol. They make all of the pizzas either round or square (i.e., Sicilian), which are baked in a pan to make a thicker, crispier crust. These square pies are baked twice—they add more sauce and cheese during the second bake—what's not to love? The menu lists seven different pies and a selection of add-ons like kale, anchovies, and roasted leeks. People who love pineapple on their pizza will be hyped when they see the "Weekend at Dino's," topped with fresh chunks of pineapple, bacon, and house-pickled jalapeños. You gotta get a side order of the garlic knots, because garlic knots are the shit and they're 99 cents during happy hour. Their bar

keeps it real and serves some solid drinks. There are about five cocktails on tap, including negronis, and that's reason enough to come here. They're pouring great wine, beer, and house cocktails behind the bar, too. Apparently it's the longest bar in Seattle. Can't tell if that's a joke or fact, but I'm laughing. If you're under 21 and can't visit Dino's, at least visit their website. It's a hilarious time portal back to sites from the 1990s, with flashing and moving graphics and a terrible visitor counter at the bottom. Then again, if you're under 21 you probably have no idea what I'm talking about, but you should look forward to the day you can eat Sicilian square pizza at Dino's.

6 BAR DEL CORSO IS A BEACON HILL GEM

Bar del Corso is like the most popular girl in school. People literally can't stop talking about her and go out of their way to see her. No really, I've never met a person who doesn't like Bar del Corso. It has the feel of a classic Italian joint—very homey.

It's a bit south in the Beacon Hill neighborhood, and there's not much else around it in terms of food or shops, but that's okay. I'd hike 8 miles up a mountain to a murder-esque cabin if that's where they were making this wood-fired pizza. If you're lucky enough to live near Bar del Corso, you've already claimed it as your own. And looking back at this list of pizza havens, I've also come to realize that great Neapolitan pizzas are not hard to find in Seattle. This one has a bit more chew than the rest and comes uncut, with a large pair of scissors. Cutting pizza is oddly satisfying. You get to determine the size of your slices, so if you're limiting yourself to two, make them big. All six of the pizzas on the menu are under $15, which is just nuts. They include everything from a simple and fresh Margherita to more involved options like the Rapini with sautéed broccoli raab, coppa, garlic, hot peppers, and smoked mozzarella. Try the Corno di Capra with house-made sausage, pickled goat's horn peppers, garlic, mozzarella, and grana cheese. These blistering pies are certainly delicious, but the small plates like fried risotto balls and ricotta-stuffed squash blossoms are what make this place a full-meal deal. Let the specials board guide you on this remarkably tasty journey; there's usually one or two pies listed and you shouldn't pass 'em up. Bar del Corso is always buzzing with neighborhood peeps, so arrive early or sit at the bar if you're on a hot date and want to avoid small children.

PUBLIC
MARKET
CENTER
MEET THE PRO
FARMERS MARKET
LOWER
MARKET
LEVELS

Pike Place Market

Eat It All and Walk It Off at the Market

THE HEART OF SEATTLE'S FOOD SCENE, OUR BELOVED PIKE PLACE Market is one of the oldest continuously operating markets in the United States. It opened in 1907 to connect farmers directly with the public, cutting out the middle man during a time when produce prices were through the roof. The ever-growing community of small business owners, farmers, and artisans is what makes this place so special. This is where locals and tourists alike touch base with the city and get their fix of its contagious energy and spirit. I'm sure you've heard of the fish-throwing dudes at the Pike Place Fish Market and the rather disgusting wall covered in chewed gum. There are more than 30 different restaurants and food stalls in the market. Foodies will feel right at home here while indulging in regional favorites like Ellenos yogurt and award-winning clam chowder. Grab a sandwich at one of the many delis or double-fist meaty hand pies from Piroshky Piroshky. You should never be walking around empty-handed.

THE PIKE PLACE CRAWL

1. **ELLENOS REAL GREEK YOGURT**, ELLENOS.COM, (206) 625-5006

2. **BEECHER'S CHEESE**, BEECHERSHANDMADECHEESE.COM, 877-907-1644

3. **PIKE PLACE CHOWDER**, PIKEPLACECHOWDER.COM, (206) 267-2537

4. **DAILY DOZEN DOUGHNUT COMPANY**, FACEBOOK.COM/DAILY-DOZEN-DOUGHNUTS-110063325682625, (206) 467-7769

5. **PIROSHKY PIROSHKY**, PIROSHKYBAKERY.COM, (206) 441-6068

6. **DELAURENTI FOOD & WINE**, DELAURENTI.COM, (206) 622-0141

1

WALK THE MARKET WITH ELLENOS REAL GREEK YOGURT IN HAND

All hail Ellenos, the yogurt of the gods. It's unlike any Greek yogurt you've ever had before. So damn thick and creamy, it feels totally indulgent yet healthy at the same time. How blessed are we to have its flagship smack dab on the corner of Pike Place and Pike Street? This family-owned yogurt is hand-crafted using pure, pasteurized whole milk sourced directly from local farms. That's what helps create the signature smooth, velvety texture and slightly sweet taste. It's sweetened with honey and offered in a variety of flavors made using 100 percent natural fruits and toppings. The rich probiotics and cultures are also a great justification for consuming this stuff on the reg. I'd spoon-feed

Beyoncé an entire tub of the Marionberry Pie Greek yogurt, that's how confident I am in this stuff. During the colder months, their Pumpkin Pie flavor is Instagrammed on average 129 times a day, chunks of pumpkin pie with the crust obviously included. Lemon Curd is a popular flavor in my household; my mom will take you down if you touch her Ellenos in the fridge. The only flavor made without local ingredients is the Passionfruit; it's sour and studded with delightfully crunchy seeds. Over the last few years Ellenos has gained a serious cult following, and now it can be found at almost any local grocery store, but none of those can match the charm of its Pike Place stand. Here, it's served piled high in a cup so

you can eat it at your leisure while navigating through the hustle and bustle of the market.

2

BEECHER'S CHEESE, PLEASE

Washington State dairy farms produce some of the world's best yogurt, ice cream, and cheese. So if we're doing yogurt right, you better believe we're doing cheese just as well. If you know cheese, you know Beecher's, famous nationwide for their handmade, award-winning cheeses and mouthwatering "World's Best" Mac & Cheese. With these headliners, Beecher's keeps Seattle's cheese game strong. The flagship store is located in the heart of Pike Place Market, where you can watch the cheesemakers hard at work while snacking on cheese curds and Dungeness crab cheese melts. There's no hesitation when lining up for a cup of their creamy mac: delectable and rich with a combination of their signature Flagship and Just Jack cheeses, penne,

and spices. Even better between two slices of sourdough and grilled, with a cup of tomato soup. There's a separate line for those who just want to buy cheese and a section in the back solely for cheese sampling. A chunk of their nutty, 15-month-aged Flagship cheese needs to go home with you. Alongside their signature cheeses is a selection of other great PNW cheeses that you should also try. If you're lactose-intolerant and thinking this cheese mecca isn't for you, take one of those magic dairy pills and go forth—it's beyond worth it.

PIKE PLACE CHOWDER IS WORTH THE WAIT

To warm our hearts and shivering bodies during the cold, wet months is award-winning Pike Place Chowder. Originally established in 1991 by a kitchen full of competitive chefs and chowder lovers. They battled it out to create chowder gold using veggies, herbs, and seafood from Pike Place Market. Not too long after perfecting their New England clam chowder, founder Larry Mellum and team traveled 3,500 miles to the Great Chowder Cook-Off in Newport, Rhode Island, where they won the title of "Nation's Best Chowder." They smashed the competition three years in a row and were later inducted into the Great Chowder Cook-Off Hall of Fame. Many awards and years later, Larry opened his first chowder house in Pike Place Market's tiny Post Alley. Since 2003, his customers travel near and far and line up to get

Skip the long lines and order online! You can select a pick-up time to ensure your chowder will be steamy hot when you arrive.

their hands on this wonderfully briny comfort food. He's mastered a handful of versions of these chunky chowders; fan favorites are the classic New England, smoked salmon with cream cheese and capers, crab and oyster with spicy chorizo, and a tomato-based Manhattan-style clam chowder. With so many small batch options on the menu, you won't want to miss out on tasting at least a few. The Four-Sampler Feast and Eight-Sampler Extravaganza are a great way to get adventurous and try a little of each. Once you find your chowder match, you can come back and get a whole lot of it packed into a giant sourdough bread bowl. Save room for at least one of the Connecticut-Style Dungeness Crab or Lobster Rolls, because they're covered in melted butter, the meat is as fresh as can be, and the bun is sweet. Without a doubt Pike Place Chowder lands a spot in the top five eats one must try while in Seattle.

4

YOU DESERVE A BAG OF DAILY DOZEN DOUGHNUTS

A bag of mini doughnuts is never a bad way to start the day. Opening early with the market every morning, Daily Dozen Doughnuts cranks out thousands and thousands of these sugar-covered gluten balls to the masses. Each tiny doughnut is carby excellence, covered in either confectioners' sugar, maple glaze (with or without bacon bits), chocolate glaze with sprinkles, or shaken with cinnamon sugar. They sell them by the half dozen and dozen—prices range depending on the type of doughnut—or you can go for the assorted bag. Their consistency is light and fluffy with plenty of air pockets, so putting down six is no problem. It's kind of fun and also mesmerizing watching the rings of dough come out of the machine and sizzle and flip in the oil. The smell of these little cake doughnuts frying wafts through the market, guiding you exactly to where you need to be. And, of course, like every other popular food stall, the lines are long. It's cash only, which is whack but worth the effort of grabbing a $20 bill from the ATM less than a minute walk away. They're served in a brown paper bag, so go off on your way to find a little hangout, a cup of coffee, and enjoy.

TIP

Go right before closing and you may score a few extra doughnuts in your bag!

5

PLENTY OF PIROSHKIES AT PIROSHKY PIROSHKY

A bakery so nice, they named it twice. Piroshky Piroshky opened their market doors in October 1992, bringing a taste of Russia to the PNW. You may be wondering what the hell a piroshky is—it's essentially a hand pie with an overwhelming variety of fillings and toppings. Each variation has been passed down from generation to generation and is as unique as the people who created them. These piroshkies are kind of legendary, and to get your hands on them, you're gonna have to wait a little (no more than 10 minutes). Do your research before you go, because once you shimmy your way in, you'll have just a few seconds to make your picks. I'll help narrow down the options for you; it's my pleasure. The menu is a split between sweet and savory. On the savory side,

The day before their opening in 1992, the owner realized that they didn't buy enough and didn't have the cash for more butter and flour. On opening morning, they found an unsigned envelope with a note and $1,000 cash inside. Turns out it was from another piroshky maker who heard about the situation and secretly donated the cash!

the Smoked Salmon Pâté is not to be missed. Inside this fish-shaped bestseller is a blend of smoked salmon, cream cheese, a dash of dill, and onion. Second most popular is the Beef and Cheese piroshky, a round pastry stuffed with delightfully seasoned beef and overflowing with cheese. The true star, in my opinion, is the Apple Cinnamon Roll piroshky: slices of Granny Smith apples dusted with cinnamon, rolled into the dough, and finished with a glaze of honey and lemon. You'll get a lot of envious looks when you walk around eating this beauty. Another sweet choice is the Oscar's Star, gracefully covered with chocolate and sweet cream cheese. Munch on your piroshkies by the waterfront or while watching the bakers make the piroshkies through the window.

6

IT'S IMPOSSIBLE TO LEAVE DELAURENTI FOOD & WINE EMPTY-HANDED

This Italian gourmet market is a foodie's dream come true. DeLaurenti has over 250 types of cheese, nine different prosciuttos, a whole upstairs dedicated to wines, an endless selection of chocolates, and every existing pasta shape in the world. Thousands and thousands of imported specialty products—you could get lost in here for hours. Whether I'm setting out for a one-stop shopping excursion for an epic picnic or just want to spend money on snacks I've never tried before, I visit DeLaurenti. An entire wall of olive oil and vinegar can be daunting, but the employees are walking food encyclopedias and will help you discover exactly what you didn't know you needed. Over at the deli, the cheesemongers are stoked to let you taste every cheese until you find what your heart desires. DeLaurenti was one of the first in Seattle to sell artisan cheeses from all over the world, so they pride themselves on having the best of the best. Next, you'll find the perfect cured meats to enjoy with your cheeses. If you're just walking through and want a little preview of what the deli has to offer, the Cone is a must-buy: a paper cone filled to the brim with cheese, prosciutto, olives, and the most addicting breadsticks. The cafe near the entrance is stocked with pastries from Macrina Bakery and Le Panier, and Caffe Umbria coffee for your breakfast needs. To avoid hangry shopping, grab an amazing cured meat sandwich or slice of their signature pizza.

TIP

Head up to the wine cellar for tastings every Saturday from 2 to 4 p.m. You can snack on your treats beside the 1,800 unique wines they source from PNW to Italy and beyond.

Queen Anne

Cupcakes & Foie Gras Cake Batter: Queen Anne Is #NextLevel

THERE ARE LEVELS TO THIS NEIGHBORHOOD. It sits on the highest hill in the city, and lower Queen Anne is the base of it all. Northwest of Downtown and home to the Seattle Center, this is where that sort of tall building called the Space Needle resides, as well as the Key Arena (RIP Supersonics) and the Pacific Science Center (the butterfly house is a trip). If I listed every attraction and event that takes place here, it'd be its own novel, but I'll name a few more: a huge food festival called the Bite of Seattle; our version of Coachella, aka Bumbershoot; interactive exhibits at the Museum of Pop Culture; and water shows at the International Fountain (originally built for the 1962 World's Fair). Queen Anne Avenue is like the backbone of the neighborhood; follow it through lower Queen Anne and straight up the hill to cover all the cool stuff. There are places to please the foodies and caffeinate my fellow coffee addicts. Start your day off with a cup of joe at La Marzocco, see what's on the rotating menu at The 5 Spot, or nosh on the finer things at Eden Hill. For a dope skyline shot, the view at Kerry Park provides. Queen Anne is considered a nicer area; most of Seattle's baller families do indeed live here. They mostly hang at the top of the hill, so it has that family vibe.

THE QUEEN ANNE CRAWL

1. **CITIZEN COFFEE**, 706 TAYLOR AVE. N, SEATTLE, CITIZENCOFFEE.COM, (206) 284-1015

2. **THE 5 SPOT**, 1502 QUEEN ANNE AVE. N, SEATTLE, CHOWFOODS.COM/ 5-SPOT, (206) 285-7768

3. **HOMEGROWN**, 2201 QUEEN ANNE AVE. N, SEATTLE, EATHOMEGROWN .COM, (877) 567-9240

4. **EDEN HILL**, 2209 QUEEN ANNE AVE. N, SEATTLE, EDENHILLRESTAURANT .COM, (206) 708-6836

5. **CUPCAKE ROYALE**, 1935 QUEEN ANNE AVE. N, SEATTLE, CUPCAKEROYALE .COM, (206) 285-1447

6. **TOULOUSE PETIT**, 601 QUEEN ANNE AVE. N, SEATTLE, TOULOUSEPETIT .COM, (206) 432-9069

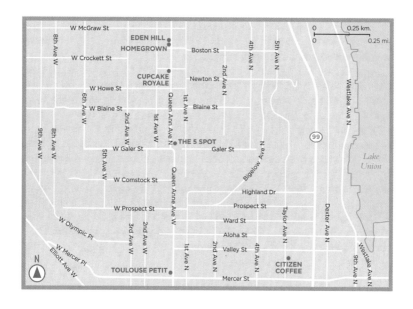

1

TURN
BREAKFAST
AT CITIZEN INTO A CREPE-EATING CONTEST

Lower Queen Anne has a ton of coffee shops, but sometimes I'm looking for something a bit more substantial than a croissant. Citizen Coffee does that whole coffee art thing—you can't help but cough up an ooh or aah. They also do that whole delicious food thing. Their crepe game is on lock. It's not every day you eat crepes, and when they're done right, they're a top breakfast food. You got your classic Nutella and your out of the ordinary strawberry-rhubarb. And for savory, crepes with smoked bacon, avocado, brie, and asparagus are happening. Biscuits 'n' gravy, huevos rancheros, and french toast also live on the all-day breakfast menu, but the Cowboy Egg Casserole in particular is what you want. They serve you about a 2-pound portion of this stuff: baked layers of corn tortillas, egg, sausage, and cheese, topped with avo, pico, and crème fraîche. Your mom would throw her casserole recipe away if she tried this. Breakfast tacos are sort of a rarity in Seattle, so if they come up in conversation, Citizen will, too. It doesn't matter which variation you choose as long as you add salsa verde. I'd be cool with the Korexican Tacos as my last meal on earth. I'm not exaggerating—they're that good. They come with bulgogi beef, pickled veggies, Mexican cheese, verde, and sriracha mayo. I wish I didn't like their Lavender Latte so much, but I do. You can grab one to go or stay. It's a pleasant place to hang while you consume all of the above. At night their patio turns into a beer garden–esque campfire party—the people love it.

2

BRUNCHIN' ALL AROUND AMERICA AT THE 5 SPOT

This one's a real Queen Anne classic—just look for the giant coffee cup sign spouting real steam from the top. The 5 Spot isn't your run-of-the-mill diner; it's the home of the "American Food Festival Series," meaning every few months their menu and decor changes depending on what region of the United States they're channeling. You're in for a surprise every time you visit. Chicago, New Orleans, Texas, the Florida Gulf . . . who knows where you'll end up? If you happen to arrive in New Mexico, you'll want to order the colossal red and green chile–sauced O.G. Breakfast Burrito. The specials are ever-changing, but the homey fare, fun atmosphere, and lively service are always on the menu. A 5 Spot Standard here to stay is the Cinnamon Swirl French Toast, a cinnamon roll–french toast hybrid drenched in house-made caramel and a whole lot of childhood memories. If that were to change, my heart would break.

Crazy for Bennies? Theirs comes on a split buttermilk biscuit. I can't find better hash browns than the 5 Spot's. If you don't order a dish that comes with them, order a side— they're spicy and perfect. Early birds and night owls can have whatever their heart desires, as most of the menu is served from early till late! We hit The 5 Spot every year for Mother's Day brunch growing up. That tradition has tragically died, but my love for their hearty diner food and spastic-themed decor lives on.

TIP

Chase away the Sunday scaries with their family-style Sunday Night Fried Chicken feast.

3

SUSTAINABLE SANDWICHES FOR LUNCH AT HOMEGROWN

Let's play it simple. Homegrown is a Seattle sandwich chain and it's really effing good. When you're in a time crunch but want something that won't make you feel like garbage, Homegrown comes through. Unlike most of America's lovely chains, they source all of their ingredients from local farms and producers. Most of this produce is grown at their very own certified organic farm in Woodinville—that's how real they keep it. Each one of their eight stores is carefully designed to be as low impact as possible. Don't go looking for a trash can, because they

use 100 percent compostable and recyclable products. If that doesn't impress you, the food will. The menu is comprised of fresh sandwiches, salads, and bowls that are super tasty and make you feel brand new. Breakfast is served all day, which is clutch seeing as I'm always in the mood for the avocado, egg, and cheese sandwich. Mornings are made sweet with the roasted banana and almond butter sandwich. The breakfast bowls with pasture-raised eggs, applewood-smoked bacon, and greens never fail me. They have many sandwiches to please any palate: chicken pesto, smoked pastrami, grass-fed steak with blue cheese, and charred broccoli with feta, to name a few. There are also vegan and gluten-free options aplenty, something delicious for everyone. Ordering from the kid's menu isn't frowned upon—the peanut butter and raspberry jam sandwich is a 10. Upgrade your life with a side of tomato soup and a gluten-free brownie. Don't forget the pickles. Sandwich environmentalism is my new passion. Health is wealth, baby.

4 EPIC DINNERS AT EDEN HILL

A fine dining restaurant the size of Kylie Jenner's handbag closet. Small but mighty, Eden Hill is one of the best things to happen to this city. Dining here is a blast. Each experience is somehow better than the last and leaves me wanting to befriend the culinary wizard behind the curtains. His name is Maximillian Petty, and he's the chef-owner and captain of the ship. A James Beard Rising Star Chef semi-finalist three years in a row (among other accolades) and a super down-to-earth guy. You'll see him back there working his magic, and it's likely he'll bring out a dish or two. His food is avant-garde, modern American, but most importantly it's exciting and delicious as hell. The chef's tasting menu changes daily and is full of surprises. It costs a pretty penny, so it's more of a celebration deal, but that's just a small part of what makes it so thrilling. Nothing you're served will make you feel dumb—it's innovative but approachable. I strongly suggest first-timers go this route. They do have an à la carte menu if you're scared of commitment. Name-drop warning: Andrew Zimmern is a fan of the Crispy Pig Head "Candybar," and you will be, too. It's one of two dishes he raves about and that you're required to order. The second is the "lick the bowl" Foie Gras Cake Batter. If you had no idea it was made of foie, you would never have guessed it.

This buttery, rich, sweet, and salty "cake batter" is served in a tipped-over bowl with olive-oil pound cake, strawberries, and sprinkles. Things will never be the same. I would change my name to Gaylord Focker for a lifetime supply of the three-ingredient Dungeness Crab Lasagna. You absolutely have to order this delicate scallop mousse and crab topped with perfectly cooked pasta, fresh herbs, and beurre blanc. Eden Hill seats just 24 people, so it sort of feels like you're eating at someone's house. That person has great taste in wallpaper and happens to be one of Seattle's most talented chefs.

See that drool worthy burger? Yeah, that's the Big Max. It's only served on Sunday night, so change whatever plans you have.

THERE'S NOTHING SWEETER THAN CUPCAKE ROYALE FOR DESSERT

Seattle's first ever cupcake shop, Cupcake Royale, is slinging some of the tastiest treats in this PNW wonderland. These made-from-scratch-daily cupcakes have the perfect ratio of frosting to cake, because there's no bigger turnoff than an excessive amount of frosting. The buttercream frosting is made using only real and premium ingredients, like local sweet butter and dark Belgian chocolate. An assortment of flavors that will rock your mf'ing socks off are offered in both gluten-full and gluten-free cakes. Forever flavors include tiramisu, red velvet, Coconut Bunny, lavender, and vegan chocolate, and seasonals like their famous carrot cake and peach bourbon crumble.

Not only are they killing the cupcake game, their ice cream is way under-rated, and most people (ahem, me) will claim it's the best in Seattle. Mashing their salted caramel and red velvet cupcakes into thick custard-like ice cream makes it's hard to knock that claim. Why have regular ice cream when you can have cupcake ice cream? All types of wild creations, best accompanied by a fresh, hand-made red velvet waffle cone, are being scooped out of this pink-and-white dreamboat cafe. Ride out this sugar high with a double shot of Stumptown coffee poured from their pink espresso machine. Both good and bad is the fact that there are locations sprinkled all over Seattle, making a sugar cleanse literally impossible.

> Cupcake Royale is not only the first cupcake shop in Seattle, originating in 2003, but the first ever cupcake store in the United States outside of New York City.

6

NEW ORLEANS LATE NIGHT AT TOULOUSE PETIT

Bringing the Big Easy to the 206 is the New Orleans–inspired Toulouse Petit. This special place has been a prime late-night spot in Seattle for a hot minute now. It's located in the party sector of lower Queen Anne and offers some amazing Louisiana cuisine till two in the morning. They have one, two, three happy hours a day, so already you have three good reasons to visit this Cajun-Creole palace. The 250 votives they light on a nightly basis contribute to the dark, sexy atmosphere. A very private setting for you and a plate of beignets to share an intimate moment. The food is outstanding and really makes you want to carve out time for a New Orleans trip. Each of the happy-hour menus overlaps a little, and with so many options they're a bit painful to navigate. But if you see things like fried green tomatoes and okra, then you're in the right place. The jambalaya is packed with house-made andouille sausage, Gulf shrimp, heat, and flavor. The "barbecued" shrimp and grits give their Southern counterpart a run for their money. I could live (and thrive) on those cheesy grits. A juicy, crispy aphrodisiac fried oyster po' boy will stimulate a strong sexual desire. Channel that energy into your buttermilk beignet make-out sesh. You'll want to coat every inch of those pillows with the Chicory Anglaise, a coffee-infused cream sauce. Round it all out with a French press coffee or fruity rum happy-hour cocktail, like the Toulouse Hurricane. Firing on all cylinders: service, energy, food, and drink—don't skip this award-winning late-night option.

THE SOUTH SEATTLE CRAWL

1. **SUPER SIX**, 3714 S. HUDSON ST., SEATTLE, SUPERSIXSEATTLE.COM, (206) 420-1201

2. **SISTERS AND BROTHERS**, 1128 S. ALBRO PLACE, SEATTLE, SISTERSANDBROTHERSBAR.COM, (206) 762-3767

3. **PHO BAC SUP SHOP**, 1240 S. JACKSON, SEATTLE, THEPHOBAC.COM, (206) 568-0882

4. **DEEP SEA SUGAR & SALT**, 6601 CARLETON AVE. S, SEATTLE, DEEPSEASUGARANDSALT.COM, (206) 588-1186

5. **FONDA LA CATRINA**, 5905 AIRPORT WAY S, SEATTLE, FONDALACATRINA.COM, (206) 767-2787

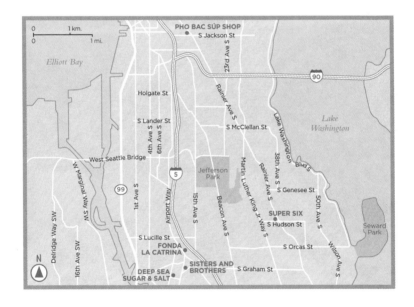

South Seattle

Journey South for Fat Noodle Pulls & Cake Slices

THE DEFINITION OF THE SOUTH END IS A BIT FLUID, BUT IN GENERAL it's a group of neighborhoods like Rainier Beach, Beacon Hill, Georgetown, and Columbia City. The 98118 is the most diverse zip code in the country and has some of the city's most overlooked yet flavorful grub. The cultures and cuisines found in these special neighborhoods are a big part of what make them so rad.

1

A SUPER BOMB BRUNCH AT SUPER SIX

When you mention Super Six, people tend to freak out. This Columbia City destination makes the same Hawaiian fusion fare that helped Marination Ma Kai blow up, but in brunch form. You cannot and will not find this food anywhere else. Feel free to hit me up if you locate another 206 establishment serving Spam sandwiches with fried eggs, harissa aioli, jalapeños, and breakfast rice. So, first things first: doughnuts and coffee. Fried balls of dough rarely disappoint, so it comes as no surprise that Super Six's malasadas made me gasp for air. These hot 'n' fresh Hawaiian doughnuts come exploding with your choice of coconut or Nutella cream (go the coconut route) and get a squeezy bottle of liliko'i (passion fruit) caramel for drizzling. You shouldn't have to pick between the pineapple corn bread and malasadas, so get both. The Big Blue Benny has patiently waited for me to realize that it's the best thing on the menu. During my last visit I fell in love with this ever-so-fluffy brioche bun topped with country ham, sautéed kale, poached eggs, and kimchi hollandaise. I'm responding to that hollandaise with four heart-eye emojis. If you don't order the chicken and waffles, you're going to be extremely jealous when you see those Hong Kong–style (egg) bubble waffles land on the table next to you. The combined textures of the bubble waffles and fried chicken will take you on the carb ride of your life. There's a sweet 'n' spicy sriracha-honey-basil situation on top. Obsessed. The loco moco makes this Hawaiian brunch thing official. You can drink as many mimosas as you want for $15, as long as you "be cool though." It has a middle of nowhere gas station aesthetic. Rustic and fun.

Super Six is super bomb and everybody knows it—make a reservation or get there somewhat early.

2

GET NASHVILLE HOT AT SISTERS AND BROTHERS

Nashville native Jake Manny is melting faces with his hot fried chicken, and it burns so good. In Georgetown and across from Boeing Field is Sisters and Brothers Bar, a divey black-and-gold-painted family-style joint schooling us on heat. This hole in the wall serves the type of spice you'll probably regret later. The chicken is so crispy and juicy, you can't stop once you've started and you'll keep coming back for more. It's sort of twisted. Pick your cut of bird: wings, tenders, white or dark meat, or a half bird. It's all served with pickles, atop a good ol' slice of white bread. (Wonder bread? Maybe.) Then, you enter uncharted territory. The spice levels are

a bit misleading, so don't get all hot and bothered when they advise you to go mild instead of hot—they're looking out for you. And if you're that asshole who thinks he can brave the "insane," get ready to pit-out your shirt in under five seconds and run to the nearest water source. This sauce is bright red from the pounds of peppers they casually throw in by the handful—I'd be curious to see where it lands on the Scoville scale. They pay extra attention to cooking the chicken, so don't be antsy; give it time. The fried chicken sandwich obviously slaps, and the sides are there to give your mouth a break from the heat in between bites. You can't dream bigger than this ooey-gooey smoked Gouda mac and cheese. Shell out the extra $2 for the house-smoked bacon chunks. Come with a friend and make sure they order the Fried Cotija Corn so you can steal one or two pieces. They also rip open a bag of Fritos and dump their house chili on it. So yeah, you want the Frito Pie. Sit inside and eat off one of the fully functioning Pac-Man tables, or outside and watch as airplanes take off and land at Boeing Field. And on a clear day you have a sweet view of Mount Rainier. If you have a thing for hella-hot fried chicken and self-inflicted torture, you'll be very happy here.

TIP

Their chicken and waffles are served during weekend brunch and will do you right.

3 PHO BAC SUP SHOP IS PHO-KING BOMB

There are a f*ck ton of pho places in Seattle, and people tend to get judgy when discussing go-to spots, so be careful and think hard before you respond. Unless Pho Bac Sup Shop is your answer, then you should be as confident as pregnant Beyoncé at the Grammys. Seattle's love affair with pho started in the International District back in 1982 when the Pham family opened Seattle's first ever pho shop. This tiny boat-shaped building originally opened as a cold-cut sandwich shop selling pho on the weekends to satisfy their Vietnamese customers' craving for this nostalgic dish from their homeland. Within that first year, the pho became so popular they ditched the sandwiches and changed their name to Pho Bac. The demand for this aromatic 10-hour broth became so high that they've since opened two other locations including their (new-ish) sister restaurant, Pho Bac Sup Shop (which is conveniently across the parking lot). The spacious Sup Shop sells their famed hot soup and a list of other fun, authentic bar snacks, including the unfortunately addicting Unfortunate Cookie Mix—a bowl of salty peanuts, chopped-up fortune cookies, and chili oil. This snack costs a single dollar. I die for the twice-fried wings the size of my left cheek (face, not ass), plump and juicy with crispy skin coated in just the right amount of fish sauce. Never do I order pho without fresh rolls, and theirs get me pumped. And now it's soup time! They have a slow-poached chicken pho that they often run out of, beef, prawn and an unexpectedly awesome veggie pho with daikon broth. The short rib pho is completely necessary if you're a first-timer or have the appetite of an offensive lineman. This bowl is huge and so are the short ribs. They get more ten-

der by the second just hanging out in there. Don't be shy; pick up those bones and suck off every last bit of meat—this is your moment. The loungy space is a bit more hip than your average pho spot, but it still honors that traditional Vietnamese flair. In the far-left dining room is a neon sign that reads Pho-cific Northwest. So cute, so smart. I kick myself every time I leave without buying a shirt.

4

CAKE FOR DESSERT AT
DEEP SEA SUGAR & SALT

Started from the Georgetown Trailer Park Mall, now she here. I'm only partially kidding—cake goddess Charlie Dunmire started selling enormous slices of cake out of an Airstream trailer on the weekends at the Georgetown Trailer Park Mall. Now, she's got a home for these layer cakes inside a historic corner grocer on Carleton Avenue. I overuse and abuse the word cute, but this little cake and flower shop is the epitome of cute. It has vintage charm for days, cards for sale and, of course, a pastry case gleaming with cake, cake, cake, cake. . . . They're sliced to order, and the layers are exposed so you can see their beautiful insides. The s'mores cake is a treat for both your eyes and stomach. Graham cracker cake, chocolate ganache, repeat—then a big,

fluffy cloud of torched meringue on top. Her 9Lb Porter Chocolate Cake lets you know she's the real deal. The darkest and moistest chocolate cake—something similar to the one that kid was forced to eat in the movie *Matilda*. Spending some time alone in my bed with a slice of carrot cake is how I prac-

This is also the site of Seattle's oldest grocery shop (since 1911), so Charlie keeps the lockers stocked with pantry essentials for the neighborhood.

tice self-care. The chunks of pineapple and cream cheese frosting really do soothe me. More and more people are realizing how nuts these Deep Sea Sugar & Salt cakes are. She sells out on the regular, so come early if you can't stand the heartbreak of there being zero slices of London Fog (an Earl Gray cake with bergamot mascarpone and cream cheese frosting) left. I'm sure the fine people of Georgetown would prefer to keep this cake on the low, so they could always have their pick of the crop.

5

LATE NIGHT MARGS AT FONDA LA CATRINA

Fonda La Catrina is a popular Georgetown stop and my absolute favorite place for Mexican food. This cantina is putting out classic Mexican dishes with slightly contemporary touches that will have you on your knees. They pair this traditional fare with a bangin' patio, margs, and tequila flights. You're getting the same service and upbeat environment as your family Mexican joint but a bit more modern experience than a casual slop of cheesy rice and beans. They keep their kitchen rocking till 12 a.m. on the weekends, and I take full advantage of this. Mmm, yes—homemade chips, salsa, and guac. As scrumptious as they may be, don't fill up on them. Not much tops a really good ceviche—theirs is exceptional and made with rockfish. Don't fill up on the chips with this one, either.

I feel all fuzzy inside when I eat the mole enchiladas. Even fuzzier while switching off bites between that and the queso fundido. The Comalito is also served with a pile of melted cheese. A hot skillet with asada, chorizo, grilled onions, jalapeño, grilled cactus, avocado, and freshly made tortillas, it's great for sharing. Tacos, tamales, tortas—three tasty wonders that all start with t. Me gusta mucho. Fonda La Catrina needs to be added to your rotation, because anyone who's searched for legit, authentic Mexican food in Seattle knows it's not easy to find.

Bonus Crawl!

Veggie Crawl
Vegans Can Have Fun, Too

SEATTLE IS LIVING LARGE WITH HIGH-QUALITY SEAFOOD, MEAT, and dairy, so we often neglect our kick-ass vegetarian options. A meatless lifestyle doesn't totally label you as a granola-eating, dreadlock-bearing hippie anymore. Turns out being healthy is becoming trendier—imagine that, people want to feel good. I love my burgers and I love my doughnuts, but sometimes I just want a big-ass salad and a break from my carnivorous ways. Plus, things that grow from the earth taste spectacular and should be celebrated. Especially since we're fortunate enough to have access to an abundance of gorgeous produce from local farms. Big shout-out to those dedicated PNW farmers—you better recognize!

THE VEGGIE CRAWL

1. **HONEY HOLE**, 703 E. PIKE ST., SEATTLE, THEHONEYHOLE.COM, (206) 709-1399

2. **NO BONES BEACH CLUB**, 5410 17TH AVE. NW, SEATTLE, NOBONESBEACHCLUB.COM, (206) 453-3233

3. **CAFE FLORA**, 2901 E. MADISON ST., SEATTLE, CAFEFLORA.COM, (206) 325-9100

4. **BOUNTY KITCHEN**, 7 BOSTON ST., SEATTLE, BOUNTYKITCHENSEATTLE .COM, (206) 695-2017

5. **FRANKIE & JO'S**, 1411 NW 70TH ST., SEATTLE, FRANKIEANDJOS.COM, (206) 257-1676

6. **AVIV HUMMUS BAR**, 107 15TH AVE. E, SEATTLE, AVIVHUMMUSBAR.COM, (206) 323-7483

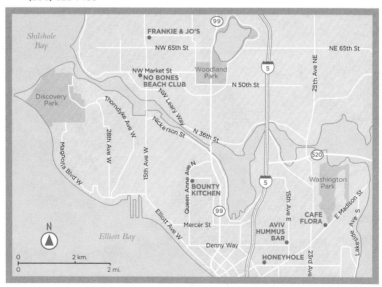

1

HANKERING FOR A SANDWICH FROM HONEY HOLE

Veg heads who are hankering for a hearty sandwich can now rejoice. Honey Hole has both meat-full and meatless sandwich offerings, but they're equally satisfying and honestly hard to tell apart. They're hot and sloppy, made with local meat substitutes and served with money sides like vegan potato salad. It's

hard to mess up here, but if you don't eventually try the Herb 'N' Cowboy, then you're blowing it hard. This monster of a sandwich is a one-way ticket to nap land. It comes stacked with a vegan Field burger, sharp cheddar, Pepper Jack, sautéed onion, classic barbecue sauce, veggie bacon, and aioli on a fresh ciabatta roll. The El Guapo is also a strong contender and more veggie focused, piled high with Roma tomatoes, red onions, green bell peppers, Italian herbs, smoked Gouda, sharp cheddar cheese, and ranch on a demi baguette. Plus, vegans don't have to lose out on the cheesiness of this one, courtesy of Honey Hole's dairy-free cheese options.

I want to personally thank them for slathering their six-hour pesto on the Emilio Pestovez, along with the caramelized onions, goat cheese, and balsamic. If you're naturally drawn to the spicy option, holler at the West Coast Blues Burger. The combination of Mama Lil's hot peppers and blue cheese makes it impossible to be disappointed. You won't miss the meat at this grungy Capitol Hill sandwich shop. I never thought I'd frequent a place for a vegetarian sandwich, but this shit is legit and my taste buds like it. It can get cramped during lunch hours, and even if you get caught in a line, it's worth it. And not to mention, there's a full bar and it's open till 12 a.m. Because vegetarians get the late-night munchies, too.

2

VEGAN JUNK FOOD AT NO BONES BEACH CLUB

I'm sure the local vegans don't want me to let the cat out of the bag on this one, but No Bones Beach Club is too good to keep from you guys. This isn't your typical garden-burger joint. Instead, this beach club is taking nutritious ingredients and creating texture-rich dishes that will shock the hell out of you. It doesn't matter if you're a carnivore or kale muncher, you will crave these flavorful plant-based creations. Their imaginative take on popular foods like poke (with beets instead of fish) and flautas (stuffed with stringy jackfruit "carnitas") will set you on a tree-hugging spree. It doesn't totally suck that some of the best nachos in the city happen to be covered in a cashew-habanero queso. And it probably wouldn't kill you to take a chill pill on the dairy consumption. This mountainous serving of Northwest Nachos is worth the addition of guacamole. Yes, we know it's extra. It always is. Of their many unique snacks and starters, I freakin' adore the Buffalo Cauliflower Wings, crisp cauliflower coated in a tangy coconut buffalo

sauce and served with a side of dill-speckled ranch. I dig the Sticky Sugarcane Drumsticks dunked in a zesty gojuchang sauce. The "bone" is made of sugarcane and surrounding it is soy protein. Very intriguing and delicious. The fries are made of eggplant and sort of resemble fish sticks. No Bones is for the vegans craving junk food and the non-vegans who are trying to make better life choices. I vibe with this "coastal inspired,"

TIP

Order the Shark Shot—this Insta-worthy drink comes topped with a toy shark and Swedish Fish.

veggie-forward cuisine no matter what weird food phase I'm in. Pssst . . . it's not all fried. There's raw salads, sandwiches, and sushi. But it's certainly all best enjoyed with tiki drink in hand. They donate a portion of monthly sales to a local animal rescue. This vegan paradise is rad. Why wouldn't you eat here?

3

CAFE FLORA IS THE OG OF VEGETARIAN RESTAURANTS

In the early 1990s, three friends converted an abandoned laundromat in the quiet Madison Valley into Seattle's vegetarian mecca, Cafe Flora. This longtime favorite continues to serve some of the most beautiful meat-free food the city has ever seen. Their eco-conscious philosophy shines through the farm-to-table fare and charming garden atrium. You're literally dining in a greenhouse, surrounded by exotic plants, a bubbling fountain, and warm natural light. Sweet corn, heirloom tomato, and Cotija cheese pizzas are among the many items that will let you forget about meat. You'll come back again just for the cheesy portobello french dip. It's served with a dipping jus far more flavorful than any beef-based jus I've had before. More importantly, it's accompanied with the best yam fries of my life. This vegetarian mainstay is a fabulous place to brunch. Highlights include a vegan Christmas-morning status cinnamon roll with caramelized sugar, maple-toasted pecans, and vanilla icing. If you look around, you'll most likely see this iconic roll on every table — It's the hottest bun on the block. The Southern Platter comes with all of the things—eggs, smoky collard greens, a house-made rosemary biscuit, and vegan country gravy. Other brunch standouts are the breakfast quesadilla, seasonal waffles, and huevos rancheros. Just about any dish can be made vegan by subbing scrambled tofu for the eggs. And for those who fear gluten, the menu is full of gluten-less options. Morning libations like melon-apple-ginger juice and Alkalizing Vitamin C Kombucha Tonic make for a healthy start. You'll feel centered af here—it's possible the serene environment and farm-fresh eats will inspire you to get in some mindful meditation.

4 FUEL UP AT BOUNTY KITCHEN

You'll feel healthier just walking into Bounty Kitchen. This upper Queen Anne kitchen boasts nutrient-dense offerings and a salted chocolate-chip cookie that puts all others to shame. The food is honest, organic, and still has that chef-driven aspect to it. Bountiful salads, grain bowls, sandwiches, and breakfast items full of flavor. Three cold-pressed juices to choose from; I swear to god these elixirs have me more wired than a shot of espresso. A quick fix to a sluggish morning. If you'd rather eat your greens thank drink them,

I'd say go with the Spicy Lemongrass Basil + Peanut salad; a slew of crunchy veggies tossed in a peanut vinaigrette. If you need something a bit more filling, the Havana Libre Bowl is the move. This one has a citrus-cashew

cream dressing and things like spinach, brown rice, sweet potato, red beans, and avocado. Hits the spot every time. They serve brunch every day, all day, so you can order the Good Morning Avocado Sandwich (their poached eggs rock), veggie hash, and gluten-free griddle cakes whenever. Pancakes for dinner? These people get me. Kombucha on tap? Sold. They get boozy, too; organic peach sangria and blueberry-mint-whiskey lemonades turn this into veggies gone wild. I kid, I kid—this is a total neighborhood spot. You'll find families popping in for a quick meal and students cramming for exams. All walks of life come to this fresh cafe to fuel up. Queen Anne, you are blessed to have Bounty Kitchen in your midst.

5

FRANKIE & JO'S CLEAN CREAM

We can't get enough of this decadent plant-based ice cream; it tastes just like the real thing. The ladies behind this vegan sensation, Kari Brunson and Autumn Martin, mastered the creamiest cashew and coconut-milk bases for their clean cream. Developing flavors on the daily with seasonal ingredients like Washington-grown strawberries and kale. Their ice cream is my preferred method of vegetable intake. They're adding superfoods and gluten-free cake and/or cookie bits to this crazy creamy base, churning out some of the best and healthiest ice cream to ever exist. I can't lie—you feel a lot better about getting your fix when you're simultaneously detoxing your liver with activated charcoal—this is where the Salty Caramel Ash gets its cool black hue. They launch new flavors monthly, while keeping crowd favorites like Tahini Chocolate and Ginger Golden Milk (colored with turmeric). Date Shake and Chocolate

Date are sweetened with nothing but California dates. They're both unbelievable. The maple, vanilla, and oat flour cones are made on the spot, so the entire place smells insane. Top your scoops off with the Salted Caramel Moon Goo—it looks like tar and tastes like happiness. Frankie & Jo's gets all of the details right—adorbs branding, Palm Springs–chic vibe, and the cactuses on the wall are clearly background models for your cone shot. When you get your cone, head to the all-weather patio in the back with pretty pink chairs and plants. They're basically forcing you to post something on the 'gram. If you get hooked, which you will, Frankie & Jo's sells their dairy-free, refined sugar–free, GMO-free creations by the pint and also ships nationally. Life is good.

6

AVIV HUMMUS BAR WILL BE YOUR NEWEST OBSESSION

You no longer need to buy the grainy stuff from Trader Joe's, Aviv Hummus Bar has introduced this city to warm, smooth, creamy, dreamy hummus bliss. What owner David Nussbaum is making tastes precisely like what you'd get in Tel Aviv, and he's serving it alongside other traditional things like pita, falafel and "cheeps." Because this is how Israelis start their day, and this is the lifestyle for me. His parents are both from Israel, he often visits the homeland for R&D, and the food here indeed reflects that. The menu lists five Israeli-style hummus variations, all served with different toppings. Classic with citrus, nutty tahini, and tender chickpeas. Add a hard-boiled egg. Just do it. I like the mushroom one sautéed with onions and another that's chunky, lemony, garlicky, and made to order. And oh my god, the pita . . . smell it. I know that sounds weird, but smell it. It's so fresh and satisfying to rip apart and mop up hummus with. If you order the falafel, just know that it's going to make you resent all the falafel you've had before. It's not overly fried—it's light and crisp, unlike the dense stuff you're used to. You can get all of this goodness stuffed into a pita if you're too lazy to build your own. Order some "cheeps" (french fries with tahini) and hamutzim (pickled peppers,

olives, and mini cucumbers imported from Israel) for the table. Their version of hot sauce is a red-pepper spread called s'chug. You'll pronounce it wrong, just like you'll pronounce hummus wrong. Depending on what you order, it's all naturally dairy-free and vegetarian. The restaurant itself is as welcoming as the people are. There's counter service for to-go orders and colorful chairs for sitting while you fall in love with Aviv Hummus Bar.

Bonus Crawl!

Seattle's Best Coffee & Bakeries
Life Is Better Baked + Buzzed

Seattle is the king of coffee. We're one of the most caffeinated cities in America. Our rich history with coffee roots all the way back to the '60s. I mean, we birthed Starbucks and now we despise it. For one, Howard Schultz sold out the Sonics, and two, we like to support small. We're into fair-trade small-batch beans from cute coffee shops and independent roasters. We have a boss coffee culture—there's a coffee shop on almost every block, and with coffee shops usually come baked goods. Our bakery scene is also thriving here—from classic doughnuts to artisan pastries. Our bakers take pride in their craft, and I take pride in overeating it.

THE COFFEE SHOPS & BAKERY CRAWL

1. **TOP POT DOUGHNUTS**, 2124 5TH AVE., SEATTLE, TOPPOTDOUGHNUTS.COM, (206) 728-1966

2. **HOOD FAMOUS BAKESHOP**, 2325½ NW MARKET ST., SEATTLE, HOODFAMOUSBAKESHOP.COM, (206) 979-2253

3. **MOORE COFFEE**, 1930 2ND AVE., SEATTLE, MOORECOFFEESHOP.COM, (206) 883-7044

4. **LA MARZOCCO CAFE & SHOWROOM**, 472 1ST AVE. N, SEATTLE, LAMARZOCCOUSA.COM/LOCATIONS, (206) 388-3500

5. **OLYMPIA COFFEE**, 3840 CALIFORNIA AVE. SW, SEATTLE, OLYMPIACOFFEE .COM, (206) 935-4306

6. **PELOTON CAFE**, 1220 E. JEFFERSON ST., SEATTLE, PELOTONSEATTLE.COM, (206) 569-4265

7. **BAKERY NOUVEAU**, 4737 CALIFORNIA AVE. SW, SEATTLE, BAKERYNOUVEAU.COM, (206) 923-0534

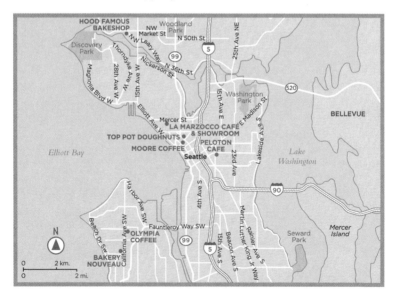

1 LIFE IS LIKE A BOX OF RAINBOW-SPRINKLED DOUGHNUTS FROM TOP POT

Doughnuts with obnoxiously unique flavor profiles appear to be the latest dessert fad. You can keep your rosemary olive-oil and curry-powdered doughnuts—just give me a maple bar. I love Top Pot Doughnuts because they're made the old-fashioned way and "hand-forged." Translation: They keep it classic, and they're not mass produced on a factory line. They have over 40 different types of doughnuts—so many choices.

This is the only place I can get a doughnut exactly how I like it and not have to mourn the loss of $5 spent on a designer doughnut gone wrong. Doughnuts are doughnuts. They should be familiar to you, and if you buy an assorted dozen, they should all be good. Buttery on the inside and crunchy on the outside Old Fashioneds and Apple Fritters (the seasonal Blueberry Fritters here are everything). The basic b*tch fall pumpkin-spice craze is inevitable, so the Pumpkin Old Fashioned is not to be skipped. Made with real pumpkin, roasted in-house. The Chocolate Cake Oreo doughnut is dipped in chopped-up Oreos. Big fan. Not many things make me happier than pink rainbow-sprinkled doughnuts do. The Raspberry Bull's-Eye is my jam (pun intended). Good doughnuts are never far—they have locations throughout the city. Their flagship shop sits on 5th Avenue in Belltown; it's a large space and a nice environment to pull out the laptop and put that sugar to use. Top Pot's hand-roasted coffee and handmade doughnuts have given me the strength to survive countless Mondays. I owe them big.

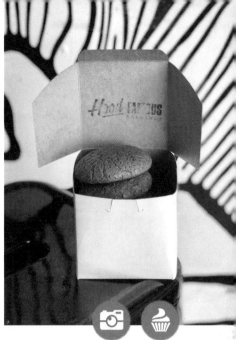

2

YOU NEED THIS PURPLE DESSERT FROM HOOD FAMOUS BAKESHOP

I'm pretty sure this Instagram-famous purple cheesecake has more followers than I do. An American dessert with an Asian twist, its color comes from the bright purple yam named ube, a root vegetable often used in Filipino desserts. The sweet yam and flaky coconut-butter biscuit crust take cheesecake to places it's never been before and put Hood Famous Bakeshop on the map. Owner Chera Amlag served this buzz-worthy cheesecake at one of her monthly dinner pop-ups, and the rest is history. The word spread fast, and this stuff became "'hood famous." In 2016, she opened a small storefront inside their Ballard production kitchen. Lucky, lucky Ballard. The cheesecake is available in a variation of Filipino-inspired ingredients and flavors like Mango Calamansi, Coconut Pandan, and White Chocolate Guava. The POG has layers of passion fruit, orange, guava—it's a stunner. Matcha fanatics will love the earthy but not overpowering Matcha Cheesecake. The Vietnamese Coffee takes the cake, though. These wonderful creations are light and creamy and bursting with flavors that you might be meeting for the first time. They're all sold in single servings or full-size cakes, if you're going big. Why not save a few bucks and try a few with the four-pack. She uses the ube in other treats, like fluffy cookies and marshmallows. Try it all—they're hood famous for a reason.

3

THE WORLD'S CUTEST LATTES ARE AT MOORE COFFEE

Moore Coffee lattes will put a smile on the moodiest of Seattleites' faces. This small family-owned cafe located in Downtown's Moore Hotel specializes in animal foam art atop hot, sugary lattes. If these fluffy bunny and Hello Kitty drinks don't cheer you up, I have a list of therapists I can recommend. You should go out of your way for one of these pretty foamy drinks and perhaps a waffle. The purple taro latte has a nutty, vanilla taste. Go green with a matcha latte. If you're like "wtf, where's the coffee?" the Mexican mocha has a bit of spice and a subtle chocolate flavor that makes the espresso go down smooth. I usually stick with the horchata latte. It has a Mayan rice base that's blended with almond extract and cinnamon. The coffee itself is up there with the other specialty coffees on this list—this isn't at all a gimmicky place. If you notice the tamales in the fridge and automatically shut the idea down, just know that they're kind of amazing and made with love. As are the waffles—there's a whole menu of them and a separate station for making and assembling. On the sweet side is the churro waffle tossed in cinnamon sugar. The caprese waffle is a tasty savory option, as is the prosciutto with cream cheese. I wouldn't plan on hanging out any longer than it takes to grab a pic and devour your purchase, as there's an endless flow of hotel guests shuffling through. The exciting part is waiting to see what design will appear on your latte. I'll take some Moore, please.

4 VIBE OUT AT LA MARZOCCO CAFE & SHOWROOM

There's nothing like the La Marzocco Cafe & Showroom—this spot is one of a kind. A trendy lower Queen Anne gathering space, it attracts coffee brats and music know-it-alls (so, almost the entire population of Seattle). Some of the best espresso shots and latte pours come out of this industrial, wide-open room inside KEXP radio station on the Seattle Center campus. Get your buzz on while sitting in comfy chairs, listening and creeping on the DJ as he or she announces songs live in the studio. The ambiance lives and breathes Seattle in its truest form—music and

coffee are basically our mascots. They host big-name album launch parties and live shows here. It's pretty dang cool. Unique in more ways than one, the La Marzocco Cafe has a rotating lineup of roasters—every few months, a featured coffee partner gets to develop a special drink menu and style up the cafe to their vision. Splurge on far-out drinks like a Million Dollar Macchiato, dipped in edible gold leaf. Or dabble in a chocolaty Sha-

kerato—espresso shaken with cream and poured over ice. If you're really, really into coffee, peep their collection of La Marzocco espresso machines. Start a GoFundMe page, because you'll really want one. In the pastry case is a small selection of baked goods from The London Plane to munch on with your coffee. The pretzel and the tahini chocolate-chip cookie both make lovely snacks. As long as the weather behaves, they keep the garage doors open—letting in hella light and fresh air. Chop it up with friends at a community table, lounge on the couches while pretending to work, or sift through records at the in-store record shop.

5

YOU'LL NEVER WANT TO LEAVE OLYMPIA COFFEE

If I lived in West Seattle, I'd be a regular here. I'd also apply for a weekend barista job because the people who work at Olympia Coffee are freakin' cool, and this little coffee shop feels like a treehouse from the future. It's modern, minimalistic, and cozy. The coffee is top tier—there's some type of sorcery going on at the roastery in Olympia. They've got me tasting coffee notes I didn't even know existed. That's because these guys are quality obsessed when it comes to their small-batch roasting. That combined with their direct trade partnerships with coffee farmers in eight countries worldwide allows more control over the flavors of coffee. These single-origin beans are available by the bag, so I wouldn't blame you if you bought one of each; they smell and taste incredible. Grab a cup to go or stay awhile in this quaint cafe. There's a ton of coffee preparations beyond just drip, and they may seem intimidating, but the baristas will help guide you to get the best taste possible. If you have a few minutes to spare, the pour-overs are the way to go. The nitro cold brew is jet fuel—it will launch you through your most dreadful of work days. Go for a house-made vanilla or honey latte and a raspberry croissant for dipping. The pastries are from local artisanal bakery Bakehouse 55, and holy shit they're good. It's full-on gluten nirvana from Everything Croissants with a cream cheese filling, caramelized sugar-coated kouign-amanns, Nutella "cruffins" and chocolate "cronuts." Olympia Coffee is my idea of a flawless cafe. I'll believe in magic once they take over this Starbucks-ridden world.

6

RIDE YOUR BIKE TO PELOTON CAFE FOR BREAKFAST BURRITOS

Capitol Hill's Peloton Cafe is repairing flats and fighting hanger. One half of this small space is dedicated as a bike shop and the other a cafe—bring your bike in for a tune-up and sip on a latte while you wait. If you're a bikeless loser like me and don't have to worry about drinking and riding, down a grapefruit Beer-mosa. I don't mind the cute boys passing through with their bikes, but the food is my reason for coming here. Chef and co-owner Mckenzie Hart has worked her way through some of the top restaurants in our food scene, and now she's got her own kitchen. She's rad, her

food's rad, I love her. Order the roasted-vegetable hash and taste the rainbow—it's loaded with over 15 different veggies. You'll die for this jerk-spiced braised brisket sandwich, unless you're vegetarian, then the veggie panini is an excellent option. But the greatest discovery here is the breakfast burrito. Holy balls—the combination of soft eggs, sweet potatoes, feta, avocado, sausage, kale, and chipotle crème fraîche is bomb af. If you know, you know. If you don't, get your ass there before everyone finds out. Cap Hill on a Saturday morning looks like a scene from the walking dead—herds of zombies packing into the nearest brunch spots. At Peloton, you can have that breakfast burrito your body is yearning for, and you don't have to wait an hour for it either. The WiFi is strong, like the coffee, and there's always an open spot for you and your laptop to set up shop. They're one of the only Cap Hill establishments that's not trying to be cool—they just are.

Taco Thursday happens from 5 to 8 p.m.—you want these chorizo, shrimp, brisket, and veggie tacos.

STOCK UP ON CROISSANTS FROM BAKERY NOUVEAU

Bakery Nouveau is like the edible equivalent of Disneyland—the happiest place on earth but also the most overwhelming. There's too much good stuff going on all in one place: specialty desserts, delicious breads, savory delights, and my favorite pastries in all of the land. They have three locations, the West Seattle being the first, so it's only right I show her love. This is the iconic bakery you make special trips to. Upon entering you won't be able to focus on anything but the smell of freshly baked bread and the gleaming pastry case. It goes on and on—you'll think you know what you want, but then you'll see something even dreamier and change your mind. The price is right here, so don't limit yourself. A box of pastries is affordable and necessary. I'd like to spend the rest of my days stuffing my face with Twice Baked Almond Croissants. I live for their crisp, flaky edges with a soft almond-cream-filled center. Feast your eyes on the berry-topped Flower Croissants. In my book, nothing's ever too pretty to eat. One of the cream cheese Danishes and almond-covered pretzel things belong in your box. There's this chocolate bread with frosting that drives me crazy. It's to die for. I always forget the name, I usually just point and that seems to work. This is one of the busier bakeries in town, so the selection dwindles by the afternoon. Get there earlyish, grab your pick of the litter and a cappuccino, and mentally take yourself to Paris for a minute.

Bonus Crawl!

Seattle's Best Bars
Barhoppin' Like There's No Tomorrow

We have dive bars, pubs, and clubs—you can get your tallboys of PBR and Rainer just about anywhere. But Seattle has a killer craft-cocktail scene with rock-star bartenders and a plethora of locally distilled spirits they play with. These bars lead the pack with all-around quality drinks, grub, atmosphere, and service. They're devoted and that doesn't go unnoticed.

THE BAR CRAWL

1. **BAR CIUDAD**, 6118 12TH AVE. S, SEATTLE, BARCIUDAD.COM, (206) 717-2984

2. **MBAR**, 5315, 400 FAIRVIEW AVE. N, SEATTLE, MBARSEATTLE.COM, (206) 457-8287

3. **NAVY STRENGTH**, 2505 2ND AVE. #102, SEATTLE, NAVYSTRENGTHSEATTLE .COM, (206) 420-7043

4. **LIBERTY**, 517 15TH AVE. E, SEATTLE, LIBERTYBARS.COM, (206) 323-9898

5. **CANON**, 928 12TH AVE., SEATTLE, CANONSEATTLE.COM, NO PHONE

6. **RUMBA**, 1112 PIKE ST., SEATTLE, RUMBAONPIKE.COM, (206) 583-7177

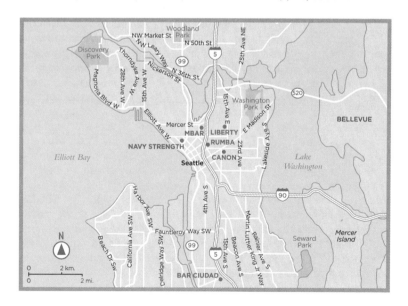

1 DAY DRINKING AT BAR CIUDAD

Bar Ciudad doubles as a chill happy-hour spot and a rowdy day-drinking destination. It's brought to you by the same guys as their grill-focused sister restaurant, Ciudad (duh, it's right next door), and Lil' Woody's. When you're not pretending like Sunday is a Saturday at one of their turnt "day-shift" parties, you'll grab a seat on the massive patio, complete with hanging string lights and colorful chairs. Order from the walk-up window (weather permitting) or inside at the bar. They specialize in rotisserie chicken and Middle Eastern mezze plates. Roll with the

friends you feel comfortable going full barbarian mode in front of—then pig out on a whole chicken. Gah, the skin is seasoned magnificently, and when you dip it in the chimichurri, you'll understand why I chose Bar Ciudad to headline this crawl. I've found that a bottle of Modelo is an appropriate pairing. The duck-fat-roasted potatoes are dangerously good. I suggest dunking them in a side of roasted garlic aioli. Dips like

TIP

Tuesdays mean all-day happy hour. Go on a Tuesday.

baba ghanoush, hummus, and smoked yogurt with chive oil come with warm flatbread for scooping. Save room for dessert, aka boozy slushies—strong af and available in rotating cocktails like hibiscus margarita and Jameson lemonade. Keep the ball rolling with draft cocktails, beer, and wine. The majority, if not all, of the aforementioned items are available for cheap during happy hour. This is another rad Georgetown joint that sits right beneath the Boeing airplanes. They're flying what feels to be right above your head, so that's a wild experience (especially when drunk).

'GRAM WORTHY VIEWS AT MBAR

2 A rooftop bar with stunning views, nosh, cocktails, and design, Mbar is a glass-walled bar and restaurant that overlooks what feels like all of Seattle—these views cannot be matched. Your experience at this sky-high bar is major, from the guided elevator ride to the carefully crafted dishes by Jason Stratton (Top Chef fans may recognize his name). The menu draws on a mix of Stratton's previous experiences, and his love for PNW ingredients and

Middle Eastern flavors. Everything is thoughtfully prepared and as attractive as the surrounding views. You can expect things like grilled trout with labneh and avocado, Persian tzatziki with pita, lamb carpaccio with figs, and falafel-stuffed peppers. The restaurant is sleek and art-driven—with statement pieces from local artists in just about every space. Even the mosaic-tiled tables are works of art. The dining room is perfect for a special occasion—count cranes and watch the sun go down while enjoying a full-service dinner.

Enjoy bites and inventive cocktails on the heated patio. It's covered so we can play on it year-round, rain or shine. Plus, there's a firepit, and artisan blankets available if you happen to get the chills. The DJs spin the hippest tunes—I've low-key Shazammed one or two songs while at Mbar. Nurse a purple drank (the Weekend Lover) while swinging in the coveted rainbow egg chair. Don't hog this chair for long, or you'll feel the death glares of people anxiously waiting to take a selfie. The happy hour is where it's at—discounted mezzes, pastas, and wine by the glass. Just make sure you rush to get here by 4 p.m. before all the Amazon employees do.

3

AIN'T NOTHING BUT A TIKI PARTY AT NAVY STRENGTH

"Some bars you date, this bar you marry."

—Navy Strength

I'm sorry but I couldn't have said it better myself. Navy Strength is my number one, and I'm ready to put a ring on it. It's a funky Belltown tiki bar with award-winning tropical cocktails from renowned bartenders Anu and Chris Elford. For a while this felt like my secret spot, but they won Best New American Cocktail Bar in 2018, and now the secret's out. Dang it. The menu is made up of three different drink categories: travel,

tropical, and tiki. Next to the drink descriptions are cartoon illustrations, so you can see exactly what you're gonna get. The special travel section changes yearly and is inspired by the flavors and service style of a different country from around the world. They'll take you to Peru with pisco and spiced purple corn beverages—each cocktail you try feels like a stamp in the passport. The "tropical drinks" look and taste like tiki drinks but aren't considered actual tiki drinks since they weren't created in a mid-1900s tiki bar. These modernized takes on tikis are made with off-the-beaten-path ingredients, like prickly pear and calamansi (a small citrus fruit). The classic tiki drinks were invented years ago by the "founding fathers" of the tiki movement. They're stiff, fruity, and never too sweet. The drinks here are so well-balanced you may not even taste the alcohol—but it's in there, and it will get ya. They even wrote a personal warning on the menu, ending with "watch your step." Chef Jeffrey Vance's eats have a tropical influence, too; refined Spam sliders, lemongrass curry with pickled veggies, and Washington albacore bites with sour pineapple. We already know you're thirsty, but come hungry.

They have three different tiki bowls for sharing. The enormous conch shell serves seven to nine people and is half off after 10 p.m.!

4 SUSHI 'N' SIPS AT LIBERTY BAR

Sushi and alcohol make the world go 'round. And it's also what makes the people cram into Liberty on a Friday night. This Cap Hill bar means business with their extensive liquor menu and scratch cocktails. Each and every cocktail is made with fresh pressed-to-order juice. That, boys and girls, is what we call commitment. This is the standard here, so you can expect the same level of detail with the sushi. I should also mention that they're open 9 a.m. to 2 a.m. and haven't closed a day since they opened in 2006. So they've broken some type of world record, right? You can have sushi on

Christmas as long as you come after 12 p.m. when sushi service begins. The menu lists different nigiri, sashimi, and specialty rolls. I have yet to meet a roll I don't like—they're bright and inventive just like the cocktails. We can all agree that making decisions is annoying—name a price and the chef will make you something nom on the spot. The veggie and cream cheese–filled Cosmic Buddha roll is topped with cashews and a sweet soy sauce. Try it. If a bottle of booze catches your eye (or sparks your interest), ask your bartender about it. They'll be more than happy to give you a taste. They barrel age their own spirits, so ask about those, too. The cocktail list is money, but it's also fun to name a liquor and let them run with it. If you're down with gin, order the Point of No Return. Your bartender will "toast" sprigs of rosemary with a torch.

Your hair might catch on fire, but oh well, at least you got a cool video. Liberty has a subtly urban-artsy vibe, but it's also cozy, even though it feels too cool to be described as cozy.

5

NEXT LEVEL COCKTAILS AT CANON

Canon is the golden child of Seattle's bar scene. I thought about copying and pasting the entire list of accolades from their website just to wow you. Nods like Best Cocktail Bar, World's Best Drink Selection and a James Beard semi-finalist three years in a row for Outstanding Bar Program. Clearly this hype isn't Instagram generated. Owner Jamie Boudreau is a booze hoarder—his collection of 4,000 (and counting) labels is one of the largest and rarest in the world. Everywhere you look are bottles (even in the bathroom), all of which you can buy pours of. But Canon is more than just a pretty bottle collection. It's a bar that is world-renowned for its innovative and ridiculously creative cocktail program. Canon goes all-out. Drinks that will make you LOL, like the bourbon-forward Whole Paycheck that comes served in

a mini shopping cart. And one that will make your mouth go numb—it's the tab of "acid" that comes with the disco-ball drink, Studio 54. It's a trip. The wild drinkware spans from vintage Nintendo cartridges to ceramic cannons spouting out "smoke." Their drink menu will make cocktail nerds feel a tingle in their pants and casual drinkers feel a tad intimidated. Let your bartender take the wheel; just shout your preferred spirit and current mood. Something like "vodka" and "over it." They always deliver. The food is up there with the drinks. I say get the beef tartare and pork belly buns. A meat and cheese board wouldn't hurt. This intimate bar leaves a lasting impression and a hit to your account balance. If you want to experience Canon, you will either wait or make a reservation online and put down a $25 deposit. They allow no more than four people in a party though, so tell Chad to kick rocks.

6

GET YOUR DAILY DOSE OF VITAMIN D AT RUMBA

Too broke for a vacay but also desperate to escape this rain before you decide to play on 405? Head to the Caribbean . . . I mean Rumba, and bathe yourself in daiquiris and empanadas. This is the Northwest's premier rum bar—explore the islands with their well-curated collection of 500-plus sugarcane rums. Rum happens to be the world's most varied spirit, with flavors from Abuelo to Zapaco. Even if you go in there with a bad attitude, insisting that you don't like rum and never will, they'll find something you deep down will dig. Ask for a "rum map" if

you're a serious rum enthusiast—tour 60 rums of your choosing and be inducted into their rum society. I'll leave all the fancy "rhum" talk to the bartenders and just fill you in on the extra special things they're doing here. The Caribbean decor is spot on. It's like a library and tiki bar had a beautiful love child. The walls are covered in collectibles and photos from the islands. Rum-forward craft drinks like punch and swizzles (tall glasses filled with crushed ice and "swizzled" with a long stick) are

TIP

Wednesday night is tiki night—get in the zone with Spam sliders and ridiculously shaped tiki drinks.

crazy good and too easy to drink. The punch drinks highlight funky rum from Jamaica and the Barbados, finished with grated nutmeg. Two thumbs up for their mai tais. Not for the faint of heart is the Red Wedding, layers of mezcal and rum with hibiscus, cinnamon, ginger, Aperol, passion fruit, and lime. By the time your third drink sets in, you'll be doing the cha-cha. Let's get some food in your system. Plantain chips with guac and fresh empanadas (get the chorizo) are a go-to. Order more than one portobello taco and definitely get the spicy shrimp ceviche. Go ahead—pump yourself with rum and vitamin D at this island retreat.

Index

About the Author

OLIVIA LARZELERE is a social media maven and the voice behind Seattle's leading food Instagram, @GrubbinSeattle. As a born and raised Seattleite, she's watched the booming tech city's restaurant scene absolutely explode and has made it her mission to keep her finger on the pulse of the 206 culinary universe. Olivia has become deeply ingrained in this ever-growing food scene, while organically growing into Seattle's most popular foodie Instagrammer and managing the social accounts of some of the city's top restaurants. She passionately supports local businesses—big  and small, old and new—and the badass people behind them. Most of her days are spent creating content for clients or exploring the Emerald City's delicious destinations (spoiler alert, this girl loves a sprinkle doughnut). Nothing makes Olivia happier than sharing these crave-worthy discoveries with Seattle's community of food lovers and the world of Instagram.